YOR

General E
of Stirling,
University of Beirut)

Ted Hughes

SELECTED POEMS

Notes by Neil McEwan

MA, B LITT (OXFORD) PH D (STIRLING)
Lecturer in English, University of Qatar

LONGMAN
YORK PRESS

YORK PRESS
Immeuble Esseily, Place Riad Solh, Beirut

LONGMAN GROUP UK LIMITED
Longman House,
Burnt Mill,
Harlow,
Essex

First published 1990

ISBN 0-582-95703-6

Typeset by Boldface Typesetters, London EC1
Produced by Longman Group (FE) Ltd
Printed in Hong Kong

Contents

Part 1

Introduction

Ted Hughes's life

Edward James Hughes was born on 17 August 1930 in Mytholmroyd, up the river Calder from Halifax, in West Yorkshire. His father William Hughes was a carpenter and veteran of the 1914–18 war. His mother, born Edith Farrar, was a descendant of Robert Ferrar, Bishop of St David's (1548–53), martyred in 1555. When Hughes was seven his family moved thirty miles south-east to Mexborough. The Pennine hills and the wild moorland above Mytholmroyd strongly influenced his imagination and he often went into the South Yorkshire countryside around industrial Mexborough, exploring and fishing. He wrote poems from an early age, at first about comic-paper heroics, later, encouraged by masters at Mexborough Grammar School, on themes influenced by the writings of Robert Graves (1895–1986). In 1948 he won a minor scholarship at Pembroke College, Cambridge (of which he is now an honorary Fellow). After National Service spent, he has said, reading Shakespeare while a wireless mechanic at a Royal Air Force station in Yorkshire, he went up to Cambridge in 1951. He studied English for two years, became dissatisfied with formal academic studies in literature, and changed to the degree course in Archaeology and Anthropology. After he graduated in 1954 he continued to frequent the university, supported by odd jobs in London (including one as an attendant in a zoo), and began to publish poems in Cambridge magazines. He and some friends started a poetry magazine, *St Botolph's Review*. It was at a party to launch this publication in February 1956 that he met Sylvia Plath (1932–63), whom he married four months later. Brilliant and sensitive, she was already known as a poet, and she began to organise the widespread publication of her husband's work, entering a collection of his poems for a prestigious competition in New York, in which it won first prize. This was the basis for Hughes's first book of poems, *The Hawk in the Rain* (1957). They lived in the United States, teaching and writing, from 1957 until 1959. When they returned they lived for a time in London, then, after the publication of Hughes's second book of verse, *Lupercal*, in 1960, in Devon, his home ever since. Their daughter Frieda was born in 1960 and their son Nicholas Farrar in 1962. Soon afterwards they separated. Sylvia Plath, who had made an attempt at suicide before she met Hughes, killed herself in February 1963.

Hawk in the Rain and *Lupercal* had been widely reviewed in Britain and in the United States. Reactions ranged from enthusiasm about a vibrant new talent to complaints about incoherence and excessive violence of thought and language. Critics interested in how Hughes would develop had to wait until 1967 for the next major book, *Wodwo*; *Recklings* (1966) — the title means 'runts' — was a limited edition of minor poems and experiments. *Wodwo* combined five prose stories and a play with forty poems, half of which had been published in periodicals between 1960 and 1963, the rest composed much more recently. The evocation of nature and especially of animals remained as vivid as in the earlier books, but the total effect was puzzling. Reviewers had already disagreed about Hughes's merit; they began to disagree about his intelligibility. In the poems of *Crow* (1970), the mocking trickster Crow shrieks protest against God and his creation. Whether or not Hughes's work was embittered by the death of Sylvia Plath and by that of his companion Assia Gutmann who died in 1969, there are extremely bleak qualities, difficult to interpret, in these books and in those which have followed.

Hughes is no literary recluse but very active, particularly in his willingness to collaborate with artists in other media. In 1960 he worked with the Chinese composer Chon Wen Chung on an oratorio (which has never been performed). His collaboration with the American engraver Leonard Baskin (1922–) has been far more fruitful. They met in 1957. In 1962 Baskin proposed that Hughes write poems to accompany his engravings. *Crow* had a Baskin cover design. At the Literary Festival at Ilkley in Yorkshire in 1975 Baskin's drawings and poems by Hughes were presented as a joint enterprise. Ten of the poems of *Cave Birds* (1975) were published in a limited edition with Baskin's engravings — some of them having been written for the drawings. The strange conjunction in Baskin's birds of human and avine characteristics has made an obvious appeal to Hughes's imagination. In 1971 he accompanied the director Peter Brook to the Fifth Shiraz Festival in Iran and wrote, for performance in Persepolis by Brook's International Centre for Theatre Research, *Orghast*, a play in an invented language, based on the myth of Prometheus. One outcome of this was the sequence of poems *Prometheus on His Crag* (1973), and another was *Gaudete* (1977), a narrative poem (first conceived as a film scenario) which was also inspired by Greek mythology. Hughes was moved by the photographer Fay Godwin's impressive studies of the Calder valley to write the poems which accompany her photographs in *Remains of Elmet* (1979). *River* (1983), which began during a fishing-trip in Alaska, alternates poems with Peter Keen's colour photographs. Work on the Devon farm of Jack Orchard, whose daughter, Carol, Hughes married in 1970, can be thought of as another sort of creative collaboration, since it led to the fine opening section of *Moortown* (1979) — poems about working on the land.

Hughes has been a prolific writer in many genres. He is a children's author: *Meet My Folks!* (poems, 1961), and *How the Whale Became* (stories, 1963), were followed by many other volumes, including the very successful fable for young readers, *The Iron Man* (1968). He is also a translator. His adaptation of Seneca's *Oedipus*, produced by Peter Brook, was first performed by the National Theatre Company at the Old Vic in March 1968. He has written (in collaboration) English versions of Hebrew verse by Yehuda Amichai (1971), and Hungarian verse by Janos Pilinszky (1976). There have been numerous short stories and plays, including radio plays, essays, reviews and talks. *Poetry in the Making* (1976) was based on his radio talks for schools. Published criticism includes introductions to collections of poems by Keith Douglas (1964), Emily Dickinson (1968) and Shakespeare (1971). Recordings of his own poetry and public readings have helped to make him widely known.

There is no general agreement about the scale of Hughes's achievement. He has won many prizes and honours, including the OBE in 1977. He was appointed Poet Laureate, on the death of Sir John Betjeman, in 1984.

General background

'Nature red in tooth and claw' is a central theme of Hughes's poetry. *In Memoriam* (1859), the great Victorian poem by Alfred, Lord Tennyson (1809–92), from which this phrase comes, contemplates the possibility that the universe is godless and that man is an animal like any other except in having consciousness of his condition. Section 55 of *In Memoriam* considers the evidence of fossils which show that many species have become extinct, and so imply that in time mankind may follow them. Tennyson asks whether Nature is careful of 'the Type' — the individual species.

> 'So careful of the type?' but no.
> From scarped cliff and quarried stone
> She cries, 'A thousand types are gone:
> I care for nothing, all shall go.'

Nature goes on to deny all knowledge of 'the spirit' other than 'the breath' of life; she gives life and death and no more. Tennyson asks whether man faces extinction, reducing to nothing all the struggles of history and faith:

> [Shall Man] Who trusted God was love indeed
> And love Creation's final law —
> Tho' Nature, red in tooth and claw
> With ravine, shriek'd against his creed —
>
> Who loved, who suffer'd countless ills
> Who battled for the True, the Just,
> Be blown about the desert dust,
> Or seal'd within the iron hills?

No more? A monster then, a dream,
A discord. Dragons of the prime,
That tore each other in their slime
Were mellow music match'd with him.

The dragons of the prime are the dinosaurs and other great reptiles of pre-
history who fought ('tore each other') in swamps; theirs would be a happier
story ('mellow music') than man's if Nature, red in tooth and claw with the
blood of prey ('ravine'), were the only law of the universe. *In Memoriam*
ends with an affirmation of the Christian faith Tennyson so nearly lost, perhaps because he could not bear to think about the bleak alternative he
expressed so poignantly in these lines. Thoughts of the alternative, made
bleaker by the possibility that extinction might come much sooner than
Tennyson imagined, have haunted modern literature, and Hughes's poetry
reflects them in various ways.

His attitudes are far removed from Tennyson's. Crow shrieks against
'the creed'. A reader's first impression of *Selected Poems* is of Hughes's
gift for imagining and describing nature at her most violent and predatory.
The hawk, the pike, the wolf and the tiger are his protagonists. He would
admire 'dragons of the prime' — and he has said that in the story of St
George and the dragon he supports the dragon. In an interview for the *London Magazine*, in January 1971, he observed that 'Christianity is just
another provisional myth of man's relationship with the creator and the
world of spirit'. He has argued in an essay on 'Myth and Education' that
'Christianity, in suppressing the devil, in fact suppresses imagination and
natural life' (*Children's Literature in Education*, 1, 1970, p.55). While
still a schoolboy he was deeply impressed by Robert Graves's argument in
The White Goddess (1948) that ancient worship of a Moon Goddess was
overthrown by the Hebrew prophets and the Greek philosophers, who put
in her place a masculine god of reason and logic. The result has been the
alienation of European culture, especially in Protestant Christianity, from
nature and the realm of the Spirit. With Graves, Hughes believes that true
poets are dedicated to the Goddess, and for him she stands for nature and
imagination, however violent, irrational or deadly.

Many other 'provisional myths' have interested and impressed him and
left traces in his poems. He respects the shamans (or witch-doctors) of
primitive religion, whom he probably first encountered when reading
anthropology at Cambridge, and believes them to have access to 'depths'
of experience in which they can identify with animals and birds. In this
respect, he has said, their role resembles that of a poet (*The Listener*, 29
October 1964, p.677). He is equally open-minded towards Buddhism and
Islam. He draws, for example, on *The Tibetan Book of the Dead* for the
central image of 'Examination at the Womb-Door' in *Crow*; and he recom-
mends the empathy of Zen Buddhism to poets, who should 'turn them-

selves into' whatever they write about. He also praises the Moslem Sufis, and alludes to their stages of personal 'annihilation' on the way to union with God, in the poem 'Stations' in *Wodwo* (*Selected Poems*, p.78), which refers more obviously to Stations of the Cross. Elsewhere in the poems there are signs of Hughes's interest in even more remote cultures, such as that of the Eskimo, and other North American myths which have influenced his conception of Crow.

Some critics have emphasised the extent to which Hughes has been influenced by the poets of eastern Europe whom he has publicised in England. These include the Yugoslav Vasko Popa (1922–), for whose *Selected Poems* Hughes wrote an Introduction; the Hungarian Janos Pilinszky (1921–) whom Hughes translated (with Janox Csokits); the Czech Miroslav Holub (1923–), and the Pole Zbigniew Herbert (1924–). Pilinszky is a Catholic who writes short, stark poems on the theme that 'God bleeds through events at times'. In the others' work no kind of faith in God or nature or humanity is to be taken for granted. Myths are to be subverted. These poets and their readers have witnessed such catastrophes in war and politics that they suspect or oppose all art which beautifies or consoles. Zbigniew Herbert's most celebrated poem is about the contest between Apollo and Marsyas who, in the Greek myth, challenged the god to a music contest and was skinned alive. Herbert's poem prefers the flayed and screaming victim to the smug god 'cleaning his instrument'. Such writing can be seen as the background to the violence and apparent nihilism in some of Hughes's work, and so can the spare language of the eastern Europeans' verse — hostile not only to poetical 'devices' but to all confident rhetoric. Hughes has written, referring to the concentration camps, that 'the silence of artistic integrity "after Auschwitz" is a real thing', since 'the human evidence of the camps has screwed up the price of "truth" and "reality" and "understanding" beyond what the common words seem able to pay' (quoted in Ekbert Faas, *Ted Hughes: The Unaccommodated Universe*, 1980, p.45). The meaningless laughter of Crow and the ambiguities of the Cave Birds reflect that kind of uncertainty.

Literary background

T.S. Eliot (1888–1965) and D.H. Lawrence (1885–1930) were the twentieth-century British writers most admired at Cambridge when Hughes was a student. The work of both appealed to him, but Lawrence's was the more congenial. Like Hughes, and unlike Eliot, Lawrence grew up in working-class England. When Hughes as a Yorkshireman refers to the southern English upper-class literary mandarins — among whom the American-born Eliot was at home — as being poorer in spirit for their 'limited' social experience, he recalls Lawrence's poetic feeling for the mining districts of Nottinghamshire. Lawrence's abandonment of the Nonconformist Puritanism of his upbringing in favour of a vaguer but equally passionate belief in 'all religions' and 'the dark gods of the blood' seems comparable with Hughes's belief in the wisdom of sorcerers and the goddess of sensuality. Eliot's Anglican creed, in which the Bible and Graeco-Roman civilisation were central, seemed inadequate to Hughes, who had a broader conception of the cultural needs of modern man. Although the young Hughes enjoyed reciting Eliot's verse, Lawrence meant more to him, and Lawrence's style of free verse rather than Eliot's has been his model. Evocation of landscapes, and their bearing on those who live with them, is a strength in Lawrence's fiction on which the younger writer drew. Lawrence, had he lived, would have praised the vitality of *The Hawk in the Rain*; it was his rule that 'the whole man alive' must enter creative writing, even at the cost of literary coherence. He would have liked the whole-heartedness of Hughes's first book and its willingness to take risks to achieve a strong effect. He would have enjoyed 'Hawk Roosting', which alarmed liberal critics, for its appreciation of essential hawkishness. Here is Lawrence's 'Snake' (*Birds, Beasts and Flowers*, 1923):

> And truly I was afraid, I was most afraid,
> But even so, honoured still more
> That he should seek my hospitality
> From out the dark door of the secret earth.

> He drank enough
> And lifted his head, dreamily, as one who has drunken,
> And flickered his tongue like a forked night on the air, so black,
> Seeming to lick his lips,
> And looked around like a god, unseeing, into the air . . .

Lawrence is impressive in his respect for the otherness of such creatures; 'secret' stresses the dark underworld where the snake, sightless in daylight, is a 'god'. However we judge Hughes in comparison with Lawrence, we must recognise an affinity between these two poets — granted that Hughes was nobody's imitator for long, and is no other writer's disciple.

Dylan Thomas (1914–53) was the most popular of the younger poets in the early 1950s. His *Collected Poems*, published in the year before he died, has a prefatory note which cites 'a shepherd who, asked why he made, from within fairy rings, ritual observances to the moon to protect his flocks, replied: "I'd be a damn' fool if I didn't!" '. That is a sentiment we should expect Hughes to approve; he says that Thomas's was 'a holy book' to him. Believing the true poet to have powers like those of the old Welsh bards, in tune with nature and the deep currents of human life, Thomas appealed to readers who felt that British verse in the 1930s has been too political and suburban. His best writing is splendidly rhythmic and evocative on big themes:

The force that through the green fuse drives the flower
Drives my green age; that blasts the roots of trees
Is my destroyer.

Or

Do not go gentle into that good night,
Old age should burn and rave at close of day;
Rage, rage against the dying of the light.

(Collected Poems, 1952, pp.9, 116)

In these poems man is seen in relation to nature and to universal facts of life and death. The young Hughes was encouraged to defy the new poets of the 1950s who held that Romanticism should have no place in contemporary culture.

This was one of the precepts of a group of poets known as 'the Movement' after the appearance—a year before *The Hawk in the Rain*—of *New Lines* (1956), edited by Robert Conquest (1917–). They were opposed to all kinds of excess, whether the intellectual and emotional wildness of Romanticism or the experiments of the 'Modernist' writers of the previous generation, led by T.S. Eliot. Poets of the Movement aimed at technical skill and intelligent articulateness about real life as they knew it in common-rooms and aeroplanes, churches, bookshops and banks—experience of a kind largely absent from Hughes's poetry. 'Neatness', 'accuracy' and 'sensitivity' are their terms of praise. They include Robert Conquest, D.J. Enright (1920–), Kingsley Amis (1922–), Philip Larkin (1922–85) and Donald Davie (1922–). They were popular, partly because they calmed readers' fears that modern verse could not be both good and fully understandable. *The Hawk in the Rain* made many reviewers—above all those who rated D.H. Lawrence and Dylan Thomas highly—regard the Movement as tame by comparison.

There has been ever since the late 1950s a mutual hostility between readers and critics who admire the poets of the Movement (a label which they have all since disowned) and Ted Hughes. Reviewing *Crow* for the *Times Literary Supplement* (8 January 1971), the poet, critic and editor Ian Hamilton (1938–) complained of lack of thought and careless diction. He has been attacked in turn by one of Hughes's champions, Keith Sagar. Hughes is not dismayed by charges of wildness. The earliest Romantics were proud of being 'wild' in spirit, and his literary antecedents are Romantic. His jaguar recalls the tiger of William Blake (1757–1827). The awe remembered from childhood in contemplating the dark pond in 'Pike' recalls William Wordsworth (1779–1850). These are great craftsmen, and Hughes is to be measured by his craftsmanship. We may regard him among the poets of this century as one ambitious to address the grandest themes—man in relation to nature, evil and death—and therefore to be judged by the highest standards.

A note on the text

Ted Hughes's *Selected Poems 1957–1981*, Faber, London, 1982, is the text which has been used in the preparation of these Notes. Dates of first publication of the poems are given in Part 2. For further details of the histories of the poems, consult Keith Sagar and Stephen Tabor, *Ted Hughes: A Bibliography*, Mansell Publishing, London, 1983.

Part 2

Summaries
of SELECTED POEMS

Poems from *The Hawk in the Rain* (1957)

Hughes chose the fifteen poems in this section from the forty poems in his first collection. 'The Hawk in the Rain' is among those omitted.

The Thought-Fox

First published in 1957, this is among the best-known of Hughes's poems. He has described, in *Poetry in the Making*, how he was sitting up late one winter night, having written nothing for a long time, when the thought of the fox came to him as inspiration, and he wrote the poem 'in a few minutes'. He added, 'And I suppose that, long after I am gone, as long as a copy of the poem exists, every time anyone reads it, the fox will get up somewhere out in the darkness and come walking towards them' (pp.19–20).

NOTES AND GLOSSARY:
prints: footprints

Song

This poem, first published in 1957, was written when Hughes was still at school.

NOTES AND GLOSSARY:
lady: the White Goddess
tipped cup: the crescent moon
foam: Aphrodite, goddess of love in Greek myth, was born from the foam of the sea
dust: because the poet is mortal

The Jaguar

An earlier version was published in the Cambridge magazine *Chequer* in November 1954. In the closing lines of that poem the people watching the jaguar are 'held' by its power which 'has not hesitated in the millions of years'; these spectators 'stare out' through the bars of the cage 'like life-prisoners'. Compare 'Second Glance at a Jaguar', from *Wodwo*.

NOTES AND GLOSSARY:

who:	whoever
mesmerized:	hypnotised, practised by Dr F. Mesmer (1734–1815)
drills:	because the eyes pierce
blind:	with rage
deaf the ear:	the ear is deafened
cell:	a monk's own room or a hermit's dwelling

Famous Poet

First published in 1957, this is a young man's attack on the kind of poet in whom 'vital fire' seems to have died. Compare 'Egg-Head' and 'The Man Seeking Experience Enquires His Way of a Drop of Water'.

NOTES AND GLOSSARY:

tankarding:	keeping alive by drinking
tissue and follicle:	the body's cells
autoclave:	sealed vessel able to contain a chemical reaction under pressure at high temperature
pyrotechnics:	firework display
bang:	inspiration
wreathed bays:	literary fame; a garland of laurel (bay) was awarded to a prize-winning poet
Stegosaurus:	a dinosaur heavily plated along the backbone

Soliloquy

This poem was first published in 1956. Compare 'Fallgrief's Girlfriends'.

NOTES AND GLOSSARY:

Soliloquy:	a speech spoken when alone
shire:	regional accent
commitments:	liability to decay

The Horses

This poem, first published in 1957, is reminiscent of nature poems by William Wordsworth.

NOTES AND GLOSSARY:

tortuous statues:	twisted shapes formed by condensation

Megalith-still:	motionless as big stones in ancient monuments
tilted:	in 'The Rain Horse', a story in *Wodwo*, Hughes notes that 'A horse sheltering from the rain generally goes into a sort of stupor, tilts a hind hoof and hangs its head and lets its eyelids droop, and so it stays as long as the rain lasts'
tear turned:	cry sharpened

Fallgrief's Girlfriends

This poem was first published in 1956. Compare 'Soliloquy'.

NOTES AND GLOSSARY:

Fallgrief:	vaguely expressive, the name was probably chosen for consonance
Index:	sign or measure
motley:	particoloured costume worn by jesters: so, folly

Egg-Head

This poem, first published in 1957, attacks the complacency of those who disregard the awesomeness of nature.

NOTES AND GLOSSARY:

Egg-Head:	the colloquial sense of 'intellectual' is not the only one intended. We are all egg-heads because our skulls are frail and self-contained, and it is natural to wish to shelter inside, living only among our thoughts and dreams
staturing:	giving stature
"I am":	the French philosopher René Descartes (1596–1650) based his system of knowledge on the formula: 'I think, therefore I am'
looming . . . earth:	the grave
whelm:	overwhelming power

The Man Seeking Experience Enquires His Way of a Drop of Water

In this poem, first published in 1957, a waterdrop on a kitchen wall symbolises the whole of dumb creation. Although it has existed everywhere and always, it is without experience or identity, and can teach no lesson.

NOTES AND GLOSSARY:

Tuscarora:	a mountain range in Pennsylvania

behemoth: monster. See the Bible, Job 40: 15
Word: divine message
quick: life

Meeting

This poem, first published in 1957, is more successful than 'Egg-Head' in treating the theme of human arrogance and our littleness in nature.

NOTES AND GLOSSARY:
Faustus: in the greatest English version of his story, the tragic drama *Doctor Faustus* (? 1592) by Christopher Marlowe (1564–93), Faustus surrenders his soul to the devil in exchange for twenty-four years of supernatural power and pleasure

Wind

In this poem, first published in 1956, the wind is a natural force before which civilisation, represented by the house, trembles.

NOTES AND GLOSSARY:
astride: as if riding, in order to drive the field through the night
orange sky: sign of bad weather to come
brunt: shock

October Dawn

This poem, first published in 1957, senses in the approach of winter the power of the Ice Ages.

NOTES AND GLOSSARY:
marigold: the flower is yellowy-orange
skin . . . ripple: the action of hoar-frost
sound by sight: seen as though alive again
Mammoth . . . Sabre-tooth: a kind of woolly elephant and a kind of long-toothed tiger, Ice Age creatures

Bayonet Charge

This poem, first published in 1957, is indebted, like the next, to stories about the 1914–18 war which Hughes heard from his father, and to the war poems of Wilfred Owen (1893–1918).

NOTES AND GLOSSARY:

In what cold . . . second?: how had destiny or politics brought him to this moment?

touchy: liable to explode

Six Young Men

This poem, first published in 1957, is another of Hughes's poems about the 1914–18 war. See the headnote to 'Bayonet Charge' above.

NOTES AND GLOSSARY:

bottom: lowest land in the valley

no-man's land: terrain between the opposing trenches

Here see: imagine

locket: it preserves a memento

The Martyrdom of Bishop Farrar

This poem was first published in 1957. Robert Ferrar, Bishop of St David's (1548–53), was burned at the stake on 30 March 1555, during the reign of Mary Tudor, the Catholic queen (1553–8) who executed some three hundred leading Protestants in this way. Hughes prefers the unorthodox spelling 'Farrar', the maiden name of his mother, a descendant of the bishop.

NOTES AND GLOSSARY:

Caermarthen: Carmarthen, a town in south-west Wales

Bloody Mary: the traditional name given to Queen Mary Tudor

red rush: fire mixed with blood

Cauterized . . . stump: as though on a severed hand

Who: anyone who

Stamp . . . current: his coins were not legal tender, that is, his Protestant words were against the law

Gave: he gave

farthing: a small coin which was worth one quarter of an old penny

miserdom of shrieks: see the bishop's words quoted in the poem's headnote

Poems from *Lupercal* (1960)

These twenty-two poems were chosen from forty-one poems in *Lupercal*.
'Lupercalia', the last poem in this collection, is among those omitted. It
refers to the ancient Roman rituals of the Lupercalia (best known today
from the first act of Shakespeare's *Julius Caesar*) in which, it was
believed, barren women were made fertile if they were struck by athletes
racing in the festival.

Mayday on Holderness

This poem, first published in 1960, meditates on violence in nature and on
war.

NOTES AND GLOSSARY:

Holderness:	the area of Yorkshire north of the Humber, between the river Hull and the North Sea
Hull:	the town of Kingston-upon-Hull where the river Hull enters the broad estuary of the Humber — into which the Ouse, the Trent, the Don and other rivers flow
Sheffield's ores:	Sheffield in South Yorkshire, a steel town, connected with the Humber by the river Don
North Sea:	at the mouth of the Humber
Birth-soils:	the boulder-clay of Holderness is, geologically, a new deposit
sea-salts:	chalk beneath the boulder-clay
pietas:	a *pietà* in painting or sculpture shows the Virgin Mary with the dead body of Christ
Gallipoli:	the Turkish peninsula where in 1915–16 British and Australian troops suffered very heavy losses. Hughes's father was a survivor of this unsuccessful campaign
beastings:	first milk from a cow after calving
anaconda:	a large South-American watersnake

Crow Hill

This poem, first published in 1958, refers to a moorland hill above the
Yorkshire town of Sowerby Bridge in the northern English Pennine Hills.

NOTES AND GLOSSARY:

The farms:	a few farmers make a hard living here
What humbles:	the persisting spirit in animal and farming life
lit:	warmed into life

A Woman Unconscious

This poem, first published in 1959, implies that one actual death means more than the worst fears of the Cold War.

Strawberry Hill

This poem, published in 1959, refers to the 'gingerbread castle', Strawberry Hill, created at Twickenham in the late 1740s and 1750s by Horace Walpole (1717–79), aesthete and man of letters. The stoat symbolises what cannot be tamed. Walpole and his house of imitation Gothic represent the civilisation of eighteenth-century England which, the poet asserts, was superficial.

NOTES AND GLOSSARY:
maskers: masked dancers
grammar: this was a great age of grammarians
corset: eighteenth-century men of fashion often wore them
Asia . . . Brixton: places remote from culture as Walpole knew it, where violence, represented by the stoat, erupts today

Fourth of July

This poem was first published in 1959, in the United States, where Hughes was then living.

NOTES AND GLOSSARY:
Fourth of July: Independence Day in the USA
Amazon: the great South American river
Columbus: Christopher Columbus (1451–1506) whose expedition crossed the Atlantic in 1492
mammoths: see the note on 'October Dawn', p.16 above
monsters: old maps pictured monsters in little-known regions
elementals: spirits

Esther's Tomcat

This poem was first published (as 'Tomcat') in 1960.

NOTES AND GLOSSARY:
Barnborough: Barnburgh, a village in South Yorkshire near Mexborough, Hughes's childhood home
Grallochs: disembowels. The term usually applies to deer

Wilfred Owen's Photographs

This poem, first published in 1959, treats a subject which Owen said inspired his poetry: 'the pity of war'. Compare 'Six Young Men', from *The Hawk in the Rain*.

NOTES AND GLOSSARY:

Wilfred Owen:	see note on 'Bayonet Charge', p.16 above
Parnell's Irish:	Charles Stewart Parnell (1846–91), a Protestant landowner, led a group of fifty-eight Irish Members in the English parliament, bringing great pressure to bear on the government
cat-o'-nine-tails:	a whip with nine thongs. Its use in the navy was suspended in 1881
Shut against:	blocked, as a door
the species:	human nature
old school tie:	a badge of status in Britain
Trafalgar:	Nelson's Column in Trafalgar Square in the heart of London commemorates the naval victory against French and Spanish fleets off Cape Trafalgar in southern Spain on 21 October 1805, which conferred on Britain sea-power and access by sea to her empire for more than a century
ship:	carry on ships

Hawk Roosting

This poem, first published in 1959, has been attacked by critics who find the poet too admiring of the hawk. See p.69 of these Notes.

NOTES AND GLOSSARY:
no falsifying dream: not dreaming

Fire-Eater

This poem, first published in 1960, was praised by Sylvia Plath, who thought it the best poem in *Lupercal*. The meaning seems to be that we are all fire-eaters because we live by the sun. In this sense even the meanest creature, such as a slug, eats the stars and is, because alive, superior to the stars.

NOTES AND GLOSSARY:
fleshed forebears: visible ancestors

Mary:	the Virgin Mary
Semele:	one of the many brides of Zeus, king of the Greek gods. She asked to see him in full glory, and the sight destroyed her
Orion:	a constellation of seven stars
Dog:	Sirius, the dog-star, the brightest of stars

The Bull Moses

This poem, first published in 1959, recalls an episode of childhood. The boy leaned into a byre and sensed both the mysterious presence of the bull in the dark and the latent power of the species, domesticated now, but wild once and perhaps in a future time to be wild again.

NOTES AND GLOSSARY:

Beyond star:	beyond consciousness
gulf:	between boy and bull
ages . . . fathers:	the past time when bulls were wild
Founding:	being founded

Cat and Mouse

This poem was first published in 1959.

NOTES AND GLOSSARY:

| two . . . four: | men or beasts |

View of a Pig

This poem was first published in 1959.

NOTES AND GLOSSARY:

| admirations: | wonders |
| this one: | this pig |

The Retired Colonel

This poem, which was first published in 1958, shows a degree of respect for the old imperialist, whose ferocious type is, the last lines say, extinct in England.

NOTES AND GLOSSARY:

| Mafeking: | during the Boer War (1899–1902) in South Africa, this town was successfully defended by British troops |

for eight months. The news of the raising of the siege on 18 May 1900 caused a night of wild excitement and rejoicing in London

Barked . . . India: the note of brutal authority in his voice was acquired in India during British rule

knout: a heavy whip (Russian, not British)

Victoria: Queen Victoria reigned from 1837 to 1901

Trafalgar: see the note to 'Wilfred Owen's Photographs', p.20 above

Wolf: wolves became extinct in England during the Middle Ages

November

This poem, first published in 1959, expresses wonder at how little separates the tramp, found asleep in a ditch, from the elements of an English winter.

NOTES AND GLOSSARY:

month of the drowned dog: when the weather seems to drown any living thing astray in it

let: an obstructed and so drier place

Relic

First published in 1958, this poem is especially good when read aloud.

NOTES AND GLOSSARY:

Continue the beginning: go on as in all past ages

but . . . devours: without devouring

cenotaph: empty tomb

An Otter

This poem, published in 1960, was inspired, Hughes has said, by a spirit using a Ouija board. The otter is a creature torn between water and land, between hunting and being hunted.

NOTES AND GLOSSARY:

vermin-poles: poles used in hunting otters

world lost: because when he took to the water he lost the happier state of being at home in one element

limpid integument: the water's surface

Witches

This poem, first published in 1958, makes a song out of traditional notions about witches.

NOTES AND GLOSSARY:

ragwort: a yellow weed
rosebud . . . bitch: women of every kind
Proprietary: owner
scowled: their ill-will injured the men they scowled at
spraddled: an invented word, perhaps mixing 'spread' and 'addled'

Thrushes

This poem, first published in 1958, contrasts the 'automatic purpose'—the unthinking efficiency—of thrush, sharks and some kinds of human genius with the labour of ordinary people distracted by fears, dreams and emotions.

NOTES AND GLOSSARY:

attent: attentive
bounce . . . second: this is how a thrush catches and eats a worm
Mozart: Wolfgang Amadeus Mozart (1756–91), Austrian composer
Orgy and hosannah: physical and spiritual extremes of experience

Snowdrop

This poem, first published in 1959, celebrates the earliest flower of the English year.

NOTES AND GLOSSARY:

wintering: hibernating
Weasel and crow: winter hunters
She: the snowdrop
this month: January
metal: able to break through the frozen earth

Pike

This poem, first published in 1959, recalls from childhood the horrid fascination of pike, seen and unseen.

NOTES AND GLOSSARY:
three inches long: when young
grin: the pike's long snout gives it the appearance of a grin
submarine: underwater; or, perhaps, resembling a submarine in silhouette; pike are freshwater fish
at this date: stressing the age of the species
monastery: medieval monasteries kept fish-ponds

Sunstroke

This poem, first published in 1959, conveys the physical impressions of losing and recovering consciousness.

NOTES AND GLOSSARY:
tunnel: vein
glared dark: the glare of the sun had darkened his vision
guns: the noise of the machine was like that of guns
damascus: steel
baby's body smoking: visualised in the shock of the moment of collapse
stone: the walls of the shed
swaddled: muffled

Cleopatra to the Asp

In this poem, first published in 1959, Cleopatra at the point of death bequeaths her world to the poisonous snake which will take her life.

NOTES AND GLOSSARY:
Cleopatra . . . Asp: Cleopatra (69–30BC) was the last of the Greek Ptolemaic rulers of Egypt; after the defeat and death of her lover Mark Antony, she killed herself by inviting the bite of an asp
bright mirror: her appearance was fascinating
Nile . . . me: she thinks of herself as Egypt
Abyssinia: Ethiopia, where the upper waters of the Blue Nile were unexplored in her time
Caesar: Gaius Julius Caesar (102–44BC), the general and, later, dictator of Rome, made Cleopatra his mistress
Pompey: Gnaeus Pompeius (106–48BC), Pompey the Great, Roman general killed in Egypt
Antony: Marcus Antonius (c.83–30BC), Mark Antony, general and joint ruler of the Roman Empire
Capricorn: constellation and sign of the zodiac, represented as a horned goat

rigid Augustus: Augustus was the title taken by Octavius Caesar (63BC–AD14) when he became emperor. Noted for his cold severity, he had intended, after his defeat of Antony, to take Cleopatra as a prisoner to Rome

virginal: he resisted her attraction

moon-horned river: a play on river, meaning the Nile, and river (from 'to rive'), meaning Antony, may be intended

bed: bed and river-bed

Poems from *Wodwo* (1967)

Twenty-eight of the poems in this section were chosen from the forty in *Wodwo*. 'Root, Stem, Leaf' and 'Stealing Trout on a May Morning' are from *Recklings*. 'Scapegoats and Rabies' is from the American edition of *Wodwo* (1967). For the title of the collection, see the note on the poem 'Wodwo', p.34 below.

Thistles

In this poem, first published in 1960, thistles are seen as reincarnations of Vikings.

NOTES AND GLOSSARY:

Icelandic: Iceland was settled by Vikings, *c.*867

Viking: see the notes for 'The Warriors of the North', p.31 below

pale hair: like that of blond Scandinavians

guttural: as in Old Norse, the language of the Vikings

feud: generations of thistles war with northern English farmers as the Viking invaders did a thousand years ago

Still Life

This poem, first published in 1961, sees the life in a flower as stronger and more lasting than rock.

NOTES AND GLOSSARY:

bruise: the blue of the harebell is unique

The Maker of the Sea: who is also the destroyer of the rocks

Her Husband

In this poem, first published in 1961, 'he' is a Yorkshire miner.

NOTES AND GLOSSARY:
her answer: she retaliates by spoiling his dinner
"Come back to Sorrento": a popular song of the 1950s

Cadenza

This poem, first published in 1964, is composed of word-pictures brought to mind by music.

NOTES AND GLOSSARY:
Cadenza: an outstanding virtuoso passage in a concerto

Ghost Crabs

This poem, broadcast as 'Nightfall' on 17 October 1965, was first published in 1966. Beginning with a description of a real seashore, it develops into a nightmare in which the human world is invaded by alien creatures. At a poetry reading in Lancaster in 1978, Hughes said that the poem was conceived as part of a play: 'The idea was that the whole world was run by a kind of angel or demon, a rather terrible kind of angel, and this is just a part to describe it' (quoted in Terry Gifford and Neil Roberts, *Ted Hughes: A Critical Study*, 1981, p.254).

NOTES AND GLOSSARY:
nacelles: engine covers
trench: like 'nacelles' a metaphor from warfare
helmets: helmet-crabs are spiders

Boom

'Bar-Room TV' and 'Wino' were first published in 1961, 'Tutorial' in 1962, 'And faces at the glutted shop-windows' ('Boom') in 1966 and 'Kafka' in 1967.

NOTES AND GLOSSARY:
shop-windows: 'Boom' in relation at least to this first section has the commercial sense of a sudden rise in prosperity and prices
dark amber: tea
mulatto: dark-skinned
Kafka: Franz Kafka (1883–1924); born in the Czech city of Prague, he wrote, in German, novels full of a strange atmosphere of uncertainty and guilt, such as *The Trial* (1925) and *The Castle* (1926)

Second Glance at a Jaguar

This poem, broadcast in 1966, was first published, ten years after 'The Jaguar', in 1967.

NOTES AND GLOSSARY:

Aztec: the dominant people of Mexico before the Spanish conquest

mantrah: a sacred text, in the ancient Indian language Sanskrit, for incantation

Cain-brands: in the Bible, when Cain murdered his brother Abel, God 'set a mark upon Cain' (Genesis 4: 15)

Fern

This poem, first published in 1967, admires small perfections in nature. This is a good example of Hughes's poems in which natural beauty is expressed in human terms.

A Wind Flashes the Grass

This poem, first published in 1966, concerns the meanings 'below words' in sounds in nature.

NOTES AND GLOSSARY:

litters downwind . . . on the air: the ploughman fears for his life, knowing that his tractor may be overturned by the wind

oracle: divine message

Bowled Over

This poem was first published in 1965. It combines two senses of the title phrase: (1) first infatuation or love at first sight, (2) death in battle. Compare 'Bayonet Charge', from *The Hawk in the Rain*.

NOTES AND GLOSSARY:

Desertion . . . bullet: desertion in the face of the enemy is punishable by firing-squad and 'burial without honours'

Root, Stem, Leaf

The sections of 'Root, Stem, Leaf' were first published in *Recklings* as 'A Match', 'On the Slope' and 'To be a Girl's Diary'.

Stations

This poem was first published in 1966. Then and in *Wodwo* it was without the third section, which originally belonged to a separate poem, 'Karma'.

NOTES AND GLOSSARY:

Stations: in the poem's context of death we may be reminded of the Stations of the Cross, the representations around a church of the stages on Christ's way to Calvary—and the devotional exercises corresponding to them. Hughes also had in mind the religious tradition in which the Islamic mystics, the Sufi, believed in stages on the way to freedom from the burden of consciousness

lifeboat coffin: the funeral service was an unsuccessful attempt to convey him to eternal life

tulip: like the blackbird in Part IV, an image which contrasts with those of death, such as the poulterer's hare and the broken neck

plantains: roadside plants whose leaves press the ground (hence 'flogged')

The Green Wolf

This poem, first published as 'Dark Women' in 1963, reflects, like 'Stations', on how close and inseparable the vitality of nature is to the horrors of death.

NOTES AND GLOSSARY:

Green Wolf: a figure in northern European myths and rituals connected with the god Balder. Hughes chose the Green Wolf as a name for death because it recalls how such ancient rites mix the ideas of green life and the wolf as a killer—ideas which blend in the poem's last lines

bloodclot: the neighbour is dying

Unmake and remake: beans, in the belief of the Greek mystic Pythagoras (sixth century BC), were associated with reincarnation

Scapegoats and Rabies

Originally a pamphlet published in a limited edition in 1967, this poem meditates on war as a pervasive fact of modern life. The victims of war are scapegoats, and those, including 'The General', who direct wars are afflicted with madness.

NOTES AND GLOSSARY:

loom: aura

millions of ghosts . . . performance: wars cause wars

Goes in . . . and out: the sound of the bullet does so literally

tête d'armée: (*French*) commander in chief of the army

Frankenstein: creator of a monster in human form in the story *Frankenstein, or the Modern Prometheus* (1818) by Mary Shelley (1797–1851)

bulled: in British-army English, shined by spit and polish

no-man's-land: see the note on 'Six Young Men', p.17 above

Notting Hill . . . Clapham: districts of London

Big Ben: the clock-tower bell of the Houses of Parliament in London.

Stealing Trout on a May Morning

The title of this poem, first published in 1964, suggests the kind of quiet Edwardian painting described in its last few lines. Hughes's description of a peaceful early morning in a trout stream is interrupted by violent thoughts of war.

NOTES AND GLOSSARY:

atrocity: the gash the car has made in the undergrowth

reeking instrument: the car

well-connected: of good family

convent: convent-school

liveried: wearing servants' uniforms

ugly petroleum: the noise of the car is ugly

sugared: the dewdrops look like sugar

goblets: the comparison with etching on glass conveys the fragility of these grasses

riding . . . roofs: the surfaces of the water

minnow: bait

alligator: the water moves as though an alligator were in it

tumbrils: army gun-carts

funeral woe-drag: as though carrying the debris of a battle

real members: the 'rout' is imaginary

trireme: an ancient Greek war-galley with three sets of oars

Theology

This poem was first published in 1961 as one in a series, 'Dully Gumption's College courses', 'Semantics', 'Political Science', 'Theology', 'Humanities'.

NOTES AND GLOSSARY:

the serpent . . . apple: the serpent does so in the Bible, see Genesis 3: 1–6

calling: in Genesis 3: 8 God's voice is heard in the garden when Eve and Adam have eaten the forbidden fruit. They hide because they are ashamed. God curses the serpent

---

Gog

This poem was first published in 1961. The biblical name Gog occurs in Ezekiel 38: 2 and Revelation 20: 8. Hughes has said that his Gog is the Dragon who represents Satan in Revelation. The Gog of the poem is excluded from receiving God's message because of an 'error' he does not recognise.

NOTES AND GLOSSARY:

Alpha and Omega: the first and last letters of the Greek alphabet. In Revelation 1: 10–11 St John records, 'I was in the Spirit on the Lord's Day, and heard behind me a great voice, as of a trumpet, Saying, I am Alpha and Omega, the first and the last . . . '

The dog's god is a scrap: see the Bible, Mark 7: 28

great bones: those of a dragon

motherly weeping: the dragon in Revelation is waiting for a woman to give birth (12: 4)

Kreutzer Sonata

This poem, first published in 1963, is an ironical attack on Leo Tolstoy (1828–1910), whose novel *The Kreutzer Sonata* (1890) belittles the place of sexual passion in marriage.

NOTES AND GLOSSARY:

Kreutzer Sonata: Tolstoy took his title from Ludwig von Beethoven (1770–1827), who dedicated his Kreutzer Sonata to Rodolphe Kreutzer, a French composer

you: Tolstoy

stabbed: in the novel a man is acquitted of murder after killing his unfaithful wife

Trukachevsky: the novel's physically attractive but caddish violinist, who seduces the wife

greed: Tolstoy, who preached chastity late in life after a spiritual crisis, had not been chaste himself.

Out

The third part of 'Out' was first published on 19 October 1963; the whole poem was first published in 1967. The first section is autobiographical, referring to Hughes's father's memories of the 1914–18 war.

NOTES AND GLOSSARY:

Out: to be out is to be away on military service

The Dream Time: the golden age, early in man's history, in native Australian mythology

Atishoo: in this surrealist part of the poem a dead soldier sneezes himself into life as a newborn baby

Remembrance Day: commemorating the dead of both world wars, this is the Sunday nearest to 11 November. Artificial poppies for buttonholes are sold in aid of needy ex-servicemen

canvas-beauty: prostitute

puppet on a wire: poppy

refreshing of ploughs: an allusion to the Bible, Isaiah 2: 4: 'And they shall beat their swords into ploughshares . . . neither shall they learn war any more'

sea-anemone: an organism, flowerlike in appearance, with tentacles which draw in its prey

New Moon in January

This poem, first published on 6 January 1963 in the *Observer*, is composed of a series of evocations of the moon, reminiscent in form as well as in subject of Japanese poetry.

NOTES AND GLOSSARY:

Shelley: the moon figures often in the Romantic poetry of Percy Bysshe Shelley (1792–1822); 'faint-shriek' is an allusion to Shelley's excited but ineffectual zeal, not a quotation

The Warriors of the North

This poem, first published in 1962, reflects on how the severe Puritanism of Calvinist Scotland developed among people descended from Viking invaders from Scandinavia. These Warriors of the North were infamous throughout the Christian lands they conquered, especially in the ninth and tenth centuries, for their pagan ferocity.

NOTES AND GLOSSARY:

anvils: the rows of bossed shields on their ships looked like anvils

envy: the Vikings attacked southern peoples richer and more civilised than themselves

disgorging of abbeys: religious-houses were commonly sacked and the monks slaughtered

casks: of wine

Gaels: Celts in Scotland and Ireland whose artists worked in gold

prolongeur: (*French*) drawing out

Calvin: John Calvin (1509–64), French religious reformer who preached a fanatical, intolerant Protestantism, most firmly established in Scotland which the Vikings ravaged and later settled

The Rat's Dance

This poem was first published in *Wodwo*. Compare 'The Howling of Wolves'.

NOTES AND GLOSSARY:

human brain: consciousness

glitterers: the stars

Heptonstall

This poem was first published as 'Hill Top' in 1965. Heptonstall is a hilltop village near Hebden Bridge, near Hughes's birthplace Mytholmroyd. Sylvia Plath, Hughes's first wife, who committed suicide in 1963, is buried in the cemetery there.

NOTES AND GLOSSARY:

geographies: migrations

sutures: seams

Skylarks

The fourth and eighth sections of this poem were added, for *Selected Poems*, to the version first published in 1966. Hughes's ideas about the birds make a contrast to those of Shelley's 'To a Skylark' (1820), one of the finest lyrics of the Romantic period. While Shelley thought of the soaring bird as a 'blithe spirit', Hughes emphasises the physical effort of the skylark's flight.

NOTES AND GLOSSARY:

Andes:	the South American mountain system has some of the highest peaks, and so thinnest air, in the world
ballast:	weight to steady a boat or balloon
sacrifices:	to the gods
gives them the O.K.:	the colloquialism is a deliberate contrast to the archaic, poetic diction in Shelley's poem
Cuchulain:	when fatally wounded, this great hero of Irish mythology tied himself to a stone pillar in order to die upright. As he died a crow settled on his shoulder
wight:	(*Old and Middle English*) creature

Mountains

This poem, first published in 1962, resembles 'Pibroch' in celebrating the 'life' of rocks.

Pibroch

This poem was first published in 1960. 'Pibroch' is the name of a form of classical bagpipe music. The poem ends by saying that here, in a place of desolate rocks and sea, is the throne of God.

The Howling of Wolves

Written soon after the death of Sylvia Plath, this was first published in 1965. Compare 'The Rat's Dance', written at about the same time.

Gnat-Psalm

This poem, first published in 1966, takes pleasure in the ethereal vitality of gnats who dance in praise of their god, the Almighty Gnat. Compare 'Fire-Eater', from *Lupercal*.

NOTES AND GLOSSARY:

Cabala:	secret Hebrew lore
crepuscular:	twilight
bodies to be burned:	See the Bible, 1 Corinthians 13: 3
Hasids:	members of a pious Jewish sect

Full Moon and Little Frieda

This poem, first published in 1963 (recorded for Argo in 1962), refers to Hughes's daughter Frieda, born in February 1960.

Wodwo

This poem was first published in 1961. The epigraph to *Wodwo* provides
the source for the name: four lines from the fourteenth-century northern
English alliterative romance *Sir Gawain and the Green Knight*. These
describe how Sir Gawain, travelling through wild country, battles with ser-
pents, wolves, bulls, bears, giants and 'wodwos which live in the rocks'.
The context implies a monster; Hughes says that his wodwo is 'some sort
of satyr or half-man or half animal, half all kinds of elemental little things,
just a little larval being without shape or qualities who suddenly finds himself alive in the world at anytime'. The speaker of this poem is such a
creature.

Poems from *Crow* (1970)

Fifteen of these poems are from the first edition, *Crow: From the Life and
Songs of the Crow* (1970). 'The Contender' and 'The Lovepet' are from the
American edition (1971). A limited edition illustrated by Leonard Baskin
was published in 1973.

Examination at the Womb-Door

This poem was first published in 1969. In the *Tibetan Book of the Dead*
Buddhist doctrine teaches that the soul succeeds in the examination at the
womb door when it fails and so avoids reincarnation. But Crow wants to
'pass' into this world.

A Childish Prank

This poem was first published together with three others; 'Crow's First
Lesson', 'That Moment' and 'Crow's Last Stand', in the *Listener*, 25
January 1968.

Crow's First Lesson *and* That Moment

These poems were first published in 1968 (see note on 'A Childish Prank').
Myths from many parts of the world account for the existence of creatures
such as sharks and mosquitoes by supposing interference in the creation of
the world by some mischievous or evil creature. Hughes has said of the
'god' of the *Crow* poems that 'he is the man-created, broken-down, corrupt
despot of a ramshackle religion, who bears about the same relation to the
Creator as, say, ordinary English does to reality' (*Crow*, Claddagh
Records, CCT 9–10, 1973).

The Black Beast

This poem was first published in 1970. Some of the Crow poems not included in *Selected Poems* also reiterate the word 'black'.

Crow and the Birds

This poem was first published in 1968. Hughes has said that 'I throw out the eagles and choose the Crow' (*London Magazine*, January 1971, p.20).

NOTES AND GLOSSARY:

Bessemer: Sir Henry Bessemer (1813–98) designed a special kind of steel-making furnace

rotovator: a mechanical plough

spraddled: this invented word also occurs in 'Witches'. Spraddling evidently contrasts with soaring, as an eagle's dawn of emerald contrasts with the Crow's garbage and ice-cream. Notice that each line has a different verb for the motions of birds.

A Horrible Religious Error

This poem was first published in 1970. The error is that of Crow who, unlike God and humanity, is unawed by evil.

NOTES AND GLOSSARY:

alibi self: the serpent is not necessarily present when it appears to be so

sphynx: in Greek mythology a monster, part woman and part lion, which posed riddles and killed those who could not answer correctly

Owl's Song

This poem was first published in 1970. Having sung the universe away, the owl ends alone and afraid of his own being.

The Contender

The theme of this poem, first published in 1971, is despair. Strongest of the strong, the contender is helpless. We might contrast the impressions of lifeless physical bulk here with the unstoppable dance of the fearless gnats in 'Gnat-Psalm', from *Wodwo*.

Dawn's Rose

This poem, first published in 1970, deals with desolation: the cry of a crow sounds without meaning in a stony world. Similes with their reminders of life emphasise the absence of life in the bird's cry.

NOTES AND GLOSSARY:
a crow: not Crow
eyelids have finished: in death
râle: (*French*) a sound from an infected lung

Apple Tragedy

This poem, first published in 1970, belongs with 'A Childish Prank' and 'A Horrible Religious Error' among Hughes's alternative accounts of the stories in Genesis. The language is as unlike the grave, poetic prose of the Authorised Version of the Bible as Hughes could make it.

NOTES AND GLOSSARY:
The serpent rested: God rested on the seventh day of Creation. See the Bible, Genesis 2: 2
goes to hell: compare this with the last line of 'A Horrible Religious Error'

Crow's Last Stand

This poem, which was first published in 1968, asserts that Crow is indestructible.

Lovesong

This poem was first published as 'Second Bedtime Story' in the *Critical Quarterly*, 10, 1968. Hughes's manuscripts show that he planned a series of bedtime stories; see Terry Gifford and Neil Roberts, *Ted Hughes: A Critical Study*, Faber, London, 1981, p.162. The love of which the poem sings is greedy and violent. Hughes has said that the poem is Crow's attempt to answer a riddling question put to him by 'a hag' during an adventure in a fairy story.

Notes for a Little Play

This poem, first published in 1969, describes two mutants alone in a Godless world, after a nuclear disaster, making love.

The Lovepet

This poem, first published in 1971, has been connected with 'Lovesong' in Hughes's account of the context in which Crow is made to answer the questions of an old woman who asks riddles. It resembles 'Lovesong' in its violent imagery.

How Water Began to Play

This poem was first published as 'Watersong' in the *New American Review*, 8, January 1970. It appeared in *Crow* with 'Fleeing from Eternity' (a poem not included in *Selected Poems*) as 'Two Eskimo Songs'. That title suggests a gentler vision—that of folklore—than *Crow* usually provides. When forced by everything to weep, water discovers its own nature.

Littleblood

The subject of this poem, first published in 1969, is the blood of life, which flows in the elephant and in the gnat—and in the poet's ear.

NOTES AND GLOSSARY:
medical: healing
Reaping the wind: see the Bible, Hosea 8: 7
a gnat's feet: compare 'Gnat-Psalm', from *Wodwo*

You Hated Spain

This poem, first published in 1970, is apparently addressed to Sylvia Plath. She and Hughes were in Spain, during the first months of their marriage, in 1956.

NOTES AND GLOSSARY:
Bosch: the pseudonym of Hieronymus van Aken (?1450–?1516), a Flemish painter, at a time when the Netherlands were ruled by Spain
spidery hand: like those of the small demonic figures in Bosch's paintings
bobby-sox: short white socks worn by young girls, hence 'innocent'
Goya: Francisco Goya (1745–1828), a Spanish artist who pictured the horrors of the French invasion of Spain during the Peninsular War
juju: an African fetish

Alicante: a Spanish resort on the Mediterranean
ferry: in Greek mythology the souls of the newly dead waited to be ferried across the river of oblivion

Poems from *Cave Birds* (1978)

These four poems were chosen from twenty-eight in *Cave Birds: An Alchemical Cave Drama*, with drawings by Leonard Baskin. See Hughes's note (p.237 of *Selected Poems*) on the relation between poems and drawings and the identities of the birds.

The Executioner

The protagonist of this poem, first published in 1974, is shown as a raven in Baskin's drawing. In the opening eight lines of the poem he is extinguishing the universe, reversing the acts of creation described in the first chapter of Genesis. Then the poem addresses the reader, so that the protagonist is 'your' executioner.

NOTES AND GLOSSARY:
hemlock: a poison. Its associations are Greek, not biblical. Taking hemlock was the usual method of suicide in ancient Greece
Across the lightless . . . water: see the Bible, Genesis, 1: 2–3, 'And the earth was without form, and void; and darkness was upon the face of the deep. And the Spirit of God moved upon the face of the waters. And God said, Let there be light: and there was light'

The Knight

In this poem, first published in 1976, the perfect self-discipline and self-sacrifice of the knightly ideal of the Middle Ages provide ironic metaphors for the disintegration of a dead crow.

NOTES AND GLOSSARY:
conquered in earth's name: he has given his body to the earth
trophies: prizes of war, that is, the parts of his corpse
vigil: a night watch, as a religious exercise
quaint courtly language: as though in medieval texts
his weapons: his bones
the sun . . . revelation: the physical universe, not God, has taken the knight. This completes the poem's mockery of traditional Christian terms

Bride and Groom Lie Hidden for Three Days

In this poem, first published in 1975, the Bride and Groom construct each other's bodies, as though mechanically, with wondering delight.

NOTES AND GLOSSARY:

two gods of mud: compare the rubble of line 2. The lovers are godlike only in the earthiest sense

The Risen

This poem was first published as 'The Sentenced' in 1974. Hughes's note on p.237 of *Selected Poems* calls this figure 'a falcon . . . a Horus', because Horus was the ancient Egyptian god of the rising sun, represented as hawk-headed. Baskin's falcon is posed impressively against a black background.

NOTES AND GLOSSARY:

apocalypse: a revelation of the end of the world
crucible: a pot or vessel in which ores are melted
land . . . wrist: when will mankind be worthy to control such a being?

Poems from *Season Songs* (1975, 1976)

'A March Calf', 'Swifts' and 'The Harvest Moon' are from the first American edition of *Season Songs*, illustrated by Leonard Baskin (1975). 'Apple Dumps' and 'A Cranefly in September' are from the first English edition (1976).

A March Calf

This poem, first published in 1973, looks at a calf's appetite for life and asks, given the common fate of cattle, why is it so eager?

NOTES AND GLOSSARY:

Little Fauntleroy: the velvet-suited hero of the sentimental novel *Little Lord Fauntleroy* (1886) by Frances Hodgson Burnett (1849–1924) is a gentlemanlike little boy
quiffed: with a lock of hair brushed down over or up from the forehead
syllogism: a logical argument in three parts
God's thumb: the calf's fate. 'Syllogism' implies that this is logically determined

Apple Dumps

This poem, which was first published in 1975, contrasts the unearthly splendour of apple-trees in bloom with a disappointing harvest of very ordinary fruit.

NOTES AND GLOSSARY:
Unearthly . . . offer: the bloom seemed supernatural
apocalypse . . . sleeper: as though to end the world with a divine awakening

Swifts

This poem, first published in 1974, celebrates the physical prowess of swifts. Compare 'Skylarks', from *Wodwo*.

NOTES AND GLOSSARY:
bolas:	a South-American missile; two or more balls connected by strings are thrown at the victim's neck
fletched:	feathered
balsa:	the lightest of woods
Apollo:	beautiful Greek god of the sun, of music and of poetry

The Harvest Moon

In this poem, first published in 1974, the moon, red from reflected sunlight, exerts her traditional magic over the countryside.

NOTES AND GLOSSARY:
doubloon:	old Spanish gold coin
petrified:	literally turned to stone; here in the sense of stilled in amazement

A Cranefly in September

This poem, first published in 1976, describes a daddy-long-legs.

NOTES AND GLOSSARY:
wain:	a hay-wagon
cannot be helped:	because the insect is too delicate to touch
calculus:	system of calculation
chitin:	the principal substance of a cranefly
armistice:	truce, during quiet autumnal weather

Poems from *Under the North Star* (1981)

This collection of poems, with watercolours by Leonard Baskin, is devoted to northern birds, including 'Goose' and 'Eagle', and animals.

Do not Pick up the Telephone

This poem, uncollected before *Selected Poems*, is unusual in having an indoor subject.

NOTES AND GLOSSARY:
Buddha: it is squat in design, like some images of the Buddha, and it is worshipped
clairvoyant: 'seeing' beyond the senses

From *Gaudete* (1977)

Gaudete is a narrative poem with forty-five short poems forming an Epilogue. See Hughes's note at the end of *Selected Poems* for the place of these poems in its scheme. They were first published separately as follows: 'Collision with the earth has finally come' (1976); 'Once I said lightly' (1977); 'This is the maneater's skull' (1976); 'I see the oak's bride in the oak's grasp' (1977); 'A primrose petal's edge' (1975); 'Waving goodbye' (1977); 'The swallow—rebuilding—' (1977); 'The glass-blade is not without' (1977); 'I know well' (1977); 'Sometimes it comes' (1977); 'Calves harshly parted from their mamas' (1976); 'A bang—a burning' (1977); 'Your tree—your oak' (1975). 'At the bottom of the Arctic sea, they say' is from *Orts* (1975).

NOTES AND GLOSSARY:
Gaudete: (*Latin*, plural imperative) Rejoice!
Arc de Triomphe: the triumphal arch in the centre of Paris which leads to the great avenue of the Champs Elysées (*French*: Elysian Fields)
stigmata: the marks of Christ's wounds which, in Roman Catholic belief, appear on the bodies of certain saints and saintly persons
metropolis: the Acropolis, the citadel of ancient Athens, a tourist attraction
strake: section
kayak: an Eskimo seal-skin canoe
Agony in the garden: Christ's night of prayer in the garden of Gethsemane in Jerusalem before his trial. See Mark 14 and Luke 22

Annunciation: the angel Gabriel's announcement to Mary that she was to be the mother of Christ. See Luke 1: 26–38

Poem from *River* (1983)

Two other poems from *River* (not *The River*, see p.51) conclude *Selected Poems*.

An October Salmon

This poem, first published in 1981, is based on thoughts about the life-cycle of a salmon found dying.

NOTES AND GLOSSARY:

two thousand miles . . . graveyard pool: salmon swim great distances to reach their breeding places, where they die

gallery of marvels: the seas

Aurora Borealis: the Northern lights; flashing lights in the sky seen in regions close to the North Pole

estuary: where the young salmon, river-born, first enter the sea

covenant: promise

this very pool: salmon return, to breed and die, to the pools in which they were born

his doom . . . heaven: compare 'The Knight', in which the knight is equally loyal to 'the machinery of heaven', in the sense of offering no resistance to death

Poems from *Remains of Elmet* (1979)

These thirteen poems were chosen from sixty-four in *Remains of Elmet: A Pennine Sequence*, with photographs by Fay Godwin. Hughes's Introduction tells us that 'the Calder Valley, west of Halifax, was the last ditch of Elmet, the last British Celtic kingdom to fall to the Angles':

> For centuries it was considered a more or less uninhabitable wilderness, a notorious refuge for criminals, a hide-out for refugees. Then in the 1800s it became a cradle for the Industrial Revolution in textiles, and the upper Calder became 'the hardest-worked river in England'.
> Throughout my lifetime, since 1930, I have watched the mills of the region and their attendant chapels die. Within the last fifteen years the end has come. They are now virtually dead, and the population of the valley and the hillside, so rooted for so long, is changing rapidly.

See also Hughes's note on *Remains of Elmet*, *Selected Poems*, p.238.

Wadsworth Moor

This poem, first published in 1978, describes the Yorkshire moorland above the Calder as a place where all living things are bound to suffer and where happiness is completely alien.

NOTES AND GLOSSARY:

Wadsworth Moor: south of Haworth Moor and north of Heptonstall, west of Halifax

star-broken: accursed

Mount Zion

This poem, first published in 1977, pictures the type of Nonconformist Protestant chapel, to be found in the Calder Valley and many other parts of Britain, and commonly called 'Mount Zion'. The chapel is seen as a deadening place, frightening to a child, in which Christianity has been corrupted. Any sign of life is regarded as a threat, even a cricket in the stonework. Compare with the atmosphere evoked in 'Heptonstall Old Church'.

NOTES AND GLOSSARY:

jibbing: shying or refusing to go on

convulsed Moses' mouthings: unpleasant ranting in Old Testament language

writhen bleeding worm: compare 'A Childish Prank', from *Crow*, which this poem helps us to understand

cobwebbed: in mourning

shaven: as the heads of prisoners were shaved

Wesley: John Wesley (1703–91), the founder of Methodism; he was a fervent inspirer of the building of such chapels

Curlews Lift

This poem, first published in 1979, tries to convey the mournful, lonely cry of these long-billed marsh birds.

Rock has not Learned

This poem, first published in 1978, is inspired by the people of the Calder region, whose sufferings are highlighted by their harsh and callous-seeming landscape.

When Men Got to the Summit

This poem, first published in 1979, imagines the reactions of modern urban men on a mountain top.

NOTES AND GLOSSARY:

Houses came . . . vertebrae slipped: the climbers' everyday world of houses and streets, and, in the metaphors, books and bodies, seems less real by contrast with the view from the mountain

Shaking their sieve: in geological time, the hills very slowly crumble

television: the climbers see the view as if it were on a television screen

For Billy Holt

This poem, first published in 1979, explores the idea of 'badlands'.

NOTES AND GLOSSARY:

Billy Holt: a self-educated weaver from Todmorden, just west of Hebden Bridge. A survivor of the 1914–18 war, he lived a life of adventure, travelling on horseback throughout Europe. He achieved fame as an author and broadcaster during the Second World War

longships: of the Vikings. See the notes on 'The Warriors of the North', p.31 above

nose and chin: of the Yorkshire people whose features are sometimes like those of the Vikings

outcast and outlaw: see Hughes's comments on the history of the Calder Valley in the note, p.42 above, on *Remains of Elmet*

hill-knowle: round hilltop

Requisitioned rain: this and the following metaphors suppose that the people made their harsh land and weather

West Laithe

This poem, first published in 1979, refers to the village of West Laithe, on the edge of Wadsworth Moor.

Widdop

This poem, first published in 1979, refers to the reservoir, named after the village of Widdop to the north of Heptonstall Moor, west of Wadsworth Moor.

Football at Slack

This poem, first published in 1979, was inspired by a soccer match at the village of Slack, close to Hebden Bridge.

Dead Farms, Dead Leaves

This poem, first published in 1979, describes the abandoned farms of the Calder Valley, no cattle now on their land.

Emile Brontë

This poem was first published in 1979. The novelist and poet Emily Brontë (1818–48) grew up, with her sisters the novelists Charlotte and Anne, in their father's parsonage at Haworth, where Emily spent most of her short adult life. She loved the moors of the region Hughes calls Elmet, usually known as 'the Brontë country'. They inspired her poems and her novel *Wuthering Heights* (1847).

NOTES AND GLOSSARY:
Crow Hill: see the note on 'Crow Hill', p.18 above
ran/The stream: the stream ran

Heptonstall Old Church

This poem, first published in 1977, expresses the central theme of *Remains of Elmet*: how the spirit of the Calder Valley has perished.

NOTES AND GLOSSARY:
bones: seen in buildings such as this church
valleys: places of human settlement

Heptonstall Cemetery

This poem, first published in 1978, refers to the cemetery where Sylvia Plath is buried. Compare 'Heptonstall'.

NOTES AND GLOSSARY:
giant beating wing: the hilltops

Poems from *Moortown* (1979)

The next thirty-seven poems are from the hundred and twenty-five in *Moortown*. The first section of this volume, originally published in a limited edition as *Moortown Elegies* (1978), is a sequence of poems written in tribute to Hughes's father-in-law, Jack Orchard, with whom he had worked at Moortown Farm in mid-Devon; it is represented in *Selected Poems* by the first group, from 'Tractor' to 'The Formal Auctioneer'.

Tractor

This poem, first published in 1978, makes the frozen tractor a creature of living metal in the mind of the farmer who battles with it and with the weather.

Roe-Deer

In this poem, which was first published in 1978, the brief appearance of two roe-deer on a snowy country road is remembered as a mysterious encounter, as though with unearthly creatures. Roe-deer are the smallest British deer.

Birth of Rainbow

This poem, which was first published in 1978, describes the Devon countryside and the late winter weather into which a calf has been born, under a rainbow.

Couples under Cover

In this poem, first published in 1978, ewes with new-born lambs resent being confined, although the brief time of shelter will give the lambs the strength they need to survive in the snow.

NOTES AND GLOSSARY:
hill-top/starts . . . stonework: unlikely disasters
a lamb grows stranger: it begins to die of cold

Ravens

In this poem, first published in 1978, a small child asks about the suffering of a 'throwaway'—a lamb which died at birth.

February 17th

This poem, first published in 1976, describes how a lamb's head has to be hacked off to free the corpse from its mother's body when it has been strangled during a premature effort at birth.

Sheep

These poems on the suffering of sheep were first published in 1974.

Coming Down Through Somerset

In this poem, first published in 1977, the ephemeral beauty of a dead badger prompts thoughts about time.

Now You have to Push

This poem, first published in 1978, is an epitaph for Jack Orchard.

NOTES AND GLOSSARY:
Masai: tall and tough cattle-grazing people in East Africa

The Formal Auctioneer

This poem, first published in 1978, is on the psychology of farmers at auctions and the skill shown there, in former days, by Jack Orchard.

From Prometheus on His Crag: 9, 10, 20

These poems, from the second sequence of *Moortown*, were written when Hughes was in Persia in 1971, and were included in the limited edition of *Prometheus on His Crag* (1973). See Hughes's note on p.238 of *Selected Poems* which refers to *Prometheus Bound*, a tragedy by the Athenian dramatist Aeschylus (525–456BC), and to the Spanish dramatist Pedro Calderón de la Barca (1600–81). In the best-known form of the legend, in Greek mythology, Prometheus made men from clay and stole divine fire to give them life. He was punished for this by Zeus, king of the Gods, who chained him to Mount Caucasus where a vulture fed daily on his liver. In Shelley's *Prometheus Unbound* (1820), a lyrical drama in four acts, he is the ultimately successful champion of mankind. In Hughes's poems he is helpless and unable to understand his predicament, godlike only in his superhuman capacity for suffering. Nothing is certain except the unthinking vulture's power to torment him.

NOTES AND GLOSSARY:
hieroglyph: a character used in ancient Egyptian picture-writing
heavenly weighing scales: Zeus weighed human issues in heavenly scales
The Knowledge: in Greek myth, Prometheus taught useful arts to mankind

From Adam and the Sacred Nine

These poems, first published in 1976 and 1977, were included in the limited edition *Adam and the Sacred Nine* in 1977; they form the last section of *Moortown*. See Hughes's note on p.238 of *Selected Poems*.

NOTES AND GLOSSARY:

Sacred Nine: here they are birds. In Greek mythology the Sacred Nine were Muses, daughters of Zeus, responsible for arts and sciences

Phoenix: a mythical bird believed to be reborn from fire, from age to age, in a nest of spices, in Arabia. A phoenix by Baskin appears on the back cover of the dust-jacket of *Moortown*

From Earth-Numb

Earth-Numb is the third section of *Moortown*. Many of the poems were previously published in the limited edition of *Orts* (1978).

Earth-Numb

This poem, first published in 1979, imagines being a hunter salmon-fishing — and being hunted by the numbing influences of earth and river.

A Motorbike

This poem, first published in 1967, has antagonised some critics normally in sympathy with Hughes's work by its assertion that life in Britain after 1945 was boring for men who had known the excitement of the Second World War.

NOTES AND GLOSSARY:

Brens: machine-guns

Bazookas: anti-tank guns

S.S.:   the notorious security forces (*schutzstaffel*) of Hitler's Germany

Swinton: a town to the west of Mexborough

Deaf School

This poem, first published in 1979, is reminiscent of D.H. Lawrence in its eager observation of the children, and in its frank, sympathetic interest in their disability.

Life is Trying to be Life

This poem was first published in 1971 as 'Crow Rambles'.

NOTES AND GLOSSARY:

the ancient mariner: in *The Rime of the Ancient Mariner* (1798), a symbolic narrative poem by Samuel Taylor Coleridge (1772–1834), the mariner is sentenced to 'Life-in-Death'. He wanders the earth, telling his tale to chosen listeners whom he holds spellbound

changeling: in folk tales, a child substituted for another, especially one left by fairies

Irish Elk: an extinct deer, known from bones found in Ireland

Speech out of Shadow

This poem, first published in 1979, is unusual for Hughes in its choice of subject, a girl's attractions. Behind them, it concludes, is a force to be expressed by one of the poet's strongest metaphors: the glare of a hooded falcon on a huntsman's hand.

Night Arrival of Sea-Trout

In this poem, first published in 1979, sea-trout (or 'salmon-trout') disturb a moonlit river on a summer night when the ancient country god Pan might be fancied running in the corn.

From Seven Dungeon Songs

These poems, first published between 1977 and 1979, form a sequence of seven in *Moortown*; they deal obscurely with large themes — Earth, nature, divinity, the integrity of the personality — using metaphors of the earth as a human body and of the body as the earth.

TV Off

This poem was first published in 1978. The man who sits over his fire, listening to the sound of the wind, was once a young soldier, glad to be alive while his comrade lay dead beside him. Now he sits up late, out of touch with the times.

Prospero and Sycorax

This poem was published in 1971 as 'Crow's Song about Prospero and

Sycorax'. Hughes's introduction to his *A Choice of Shakespeare's Verse* (1971) argues that in *The Tempest* Shakespeare made his magician-lord Prospero the opponent of the witch Sycorax because he saw her as the representative of the White Goddess, subversive of male, rational rule in the world.

NOTES AND GLOSSARY:

She: a witch, the mother of Caliban in *The Tempest*

Ophelia: in Shakespeare's *Hamlet* the girl rejected by Hamlet, who loses her reason and drowns herself

swallowed him: swallowed Hamlet

George: Hughes holds that Saint George, the traditional dragon-slayer, represents Christianity at its worst, hostile to the imagination and to the White Goddess

Jocasta: the mother of Oedipus in ancient Greek legend

He prefers: Oedipus put out his own eyes when he learned that he had killed his father Laius and married his own mother

Cordelia: in Shakespeare's *King Lear*, the rejected but ever-loving daughter of Lear

not himself: Lear, who loses his reason

Tiger-Psalm

This poem was first published in 1969 as 'Crow's Table Talk'. The machine-guns, representing war, are contrasted with the tiger which kills naturally. Line 32 of the 1969 version reads: 'Kills with the strength of madness, kills possessed.' The revision adds dignity to the tiger.

NOTES AND GLOSSARY:

Acropolis: the ancient citadel of Athens

a to-fro dialectic: thesis is followed by antithesis in this system of argument

Himalayas: the mountains which divide the Indian subcontinent from Asia

Ganges: the great river which flows south-east from the Himalayan mountains across northern India. These places are chosen because they are beautiful, sacred and tiger-country

---

The Stone

In this poem, first published in 1974, the gravestone is used to place death in a geological perspective.

The Woman in the Valley

In this poem, first published in 1981, 'the woman in the valley' is the river.

A God

This poem, first published in 1974, reworks themes familiar from many earlier poems. Compare 'Prometheus on His Crag', from *Moortown*.

NOTES AND GLOSSARY:
parietals: bones in the skull

Two poems from *River* (1983)

Projected as *The River* and so named in *Selected Poems*, *River*, with photographs by P. Keen, is a sequence of river poems, composed after a fishing trip in Alaska.

Salmon Eggs

This poem, first published in 1981, has two themes: that '*Only birth matters*' in nature, and that the permanence of the river makes death seem 'a superficiality'.

NOTES AND GLOSSARY:
deathwards: see the notes on 'An October Salmon', p.42 above
Mastodon: extinct animal of the elephant kind
Sanctus Sanctus: (*Latin*) Holy, Holy; see the Bible, Isaiah 6: 3

That Morning

First published in 1981, this poem concludes the volume with a beatific experience of a salmon-crowded river in Alaska.

NOTES AND GLOSSARY:
far-aimed . . . map: salmon travel far from the river where they are born
Lancasters: bomber aircraft used in the Second World War

Part 3

Commentary

A modern Aesop

One critic has called Hughes 'a kind of twentieth-century Aesop' (Stan Smith, see Part 5). This is a good starting-point because it reminds us that there is a long and widespread tradition of literature dealing with animals but full of human interest. Aesop was a Greek of the sixth century BC; the animal fables attributed to him have been rewritten, in simple and sophisticated versions, in every period since the Middle Ages. Hughes is the most recent of English writers to draw upon the richly creative possibilities to be found in comparisons between mankind and the rest of the animal world.

This kind of writing is anthropomorphic. The term derives from the Greek words for 'man' and 'form'; it means having human characteristics. Aesop's beasts behave like people: the boastful hare challenges the tortoise to a race; the cunning fox flatters the cock. Above all, the animals of fables are able to talk. This convention links Aesop's genre with other kinds of literature in which dumb creatures are endowed with language. These too have been written since antiquity. In the play *The Birds* by the Athenian comic dramatist Aristophanes (*c*.448–*c*.380BC), a chorus of birds sings in beautiful words of its sympathy with the sufferings of earthbound humanity. Eighteen hundred years later, in *The Parliament of Fowls* by Geoffrey Chaucer (*c*.1340–*c*. 1400), an assembly of birds formally debates medieval matters in late Middle English verse. A few centuries later, the Romantic poets felt birdsong to be ecstatic. In his 'Ode to a Nightingale' (1819), John Keats (1795–1821) hears in the notes of a nightingale a song of triumph over human suffering and mortality, and his poem speaks to the bird while it sings of summer. The nightingale for Keats, the skylark for Shelley, and the tiger ('burning bright / In the forests of the night') for William Blake, were symbols to convey what birds and animals represent in all ages: our longing for degrees of freedom, strength and beauty beyond human limitations. Keats and Shelley singing back to the birds, Blake interrogating the tiger, and other poets using birds and animals for other purposes, enjoy the same licence as writers of fables, to pretend that animals share our language, and so to pretend that they share our experience.

There are various ways in which animals and other creatures in the poems can be said to share language with us. Crow can talk about anything. He is, as we shall see, anthropomorphic in another sense, because he is a supernatural character with human attributes; but he is a character, and if the poems succeed in making us suspend our disbelief in him we are prepared to hear him talk, to God or the devil, as Hughes might talk himself. When the hawk speaks, in 'Hawk Roosting', however, we interpret its words on another level of the imagination. While Crow belongs to the realms of fantasy and is akin to the creations of Aesop and Walt Disney, the hawk is more truly a hawk and speaks in looks and action—even in its immobility—with meanings which the poem puts into words:

I kill where I please because it is all mine.

I am going to keep things like this.

Such statements (these lines are from the fourth and last stanzas of 'Hawk Roosting') correspond to attitudes—aggressive and conservative—which we think of as hawk-like. If Crow is a bird treated as a human character, the hawk is a bird which resembles and can represent a human type. At an extreme from the Crow poems, and far more realistic, are the lambs of 'Sheep', whose bleatings are easy to translate:

Mother Mother Mother the lambs
Are crying

The lambs are allowed only one word, but it humanises them in an entirely traditional way. Hughes, of course, is not always traditional; but gnats which sing hymns, curlews which weep, tigers which bless, rats which scream, the cricket which makes music, and even the March calf with its eloquent Moo, have received what literature has always given to animals: language, in which we can pretend to understand them so that we can talk more effectively about ourselves.

There are various ways in which Hughes's animals, birds, fish, reptiles, insects and creatures of indeterminate species such as a wodwo or a fire-eater are anthropomorphised. They need not talk to be brought within our terms of understanding. Hughes is, of course, quite unlike Aesop in his scientific interest—in the life cycle of a salmon or the musculature of a skylark. Such concerns are usually subordinated to themes of human interest. Metaphor and symbol bring salmon or skylark within human points of view, seeking to establish what these creatures share with us and how they are alien and mysterious. Hughes is very good at describing a fish dying in a pool of water or a bird thrusting itself skywards with straining wings, so that we imagine states of being which are like and unlike our own. It is because he does this so well that he can convey his themes—of death in the salmon, and vitality in the skylark, and of their inseparability—with novelty and force. He has an instinct for writing about animals, so that our attempts to classify his poems by topics are thwarted: some are about people, but the colonel in 'The Retired Colonel' pales in company with 'the last English Wolf . . . And the last sturgeon of Thames'; some are about landscapes, but many readers of *Remains of Elmet* remember even better than the Yorkshire terrain described there, the wildlife:

> The birds, beautiful-eyed, with soft cries,
> The cattle of heaven . . .

who 'visit' the empty lands in 'Dead Farms, Dead Leaves'; some are about history, but from them we remember best the stoat in 'Strawberry Hill' (from *Lupercal*); in those which are mythic, Prometheus seems less grand and mysterious than the sluglike hero of 'Fire-Eater' (from *Lupercal*) crawling among fronds but eating the stars. In this respect, too, we can think of Hughes as an heir of Aesop, without meaning that he writes fables. His writing brings animals to life, but it concerns us.

Several poems in *The Hawk in the Rain* make symbols of animals which are described from observation. Hughes chose to set 'The Thought-Fox' at the head of *Selected Poems* because it is a guide to the ambiguous nature of animals in his work. He has commented that the subject is 'a fox that is both a fox and not a fox'. Much has been published in critical studies to enlarge on that. The poem is attractive in the simplicity of its scheme, contrasting the nose, paws and eye of the intruder in the dark with the abstract idea for a poem, and cunningly surprising us with a physical fox which is cold and distant, while its metaphorical counterpart enters the poet's head — and the reader's — 'with a sudden sharp hot stink of fox'. We are meant to think about relations between the fox in the snow and the fox on the page, and to wonder where the second fox came from. Perhaps there are holes in the head through which beasts jump out of the subconscious. 'The Jaguar' is another poem among those selected from *The Hawk in the Rain* which creates a symbol from a vivid description of a real animal. Notice the verb 'spins' in line 16, which conveys the jaguar's mobility, after the succession of words dwelling on its bulky strength. The physical creature spins from the bars because it is caged; its energy and determination seem uncageable, and in the last stanza the world's horizons persuade us that the crowd of zoo-goers are the ones confined. In 'Meeting', also from *The Hawk in the Rain*, a goat looks down from a hillside with a stare that the climber can never forget. Posing grandly before a mirror, later in life, the same man remembers the goat's yellow eye, devil's head, clattering hooves, and the sense of mystery which accompanied these impressions — and he feels belittled. The goat's compelling eye may remind us of the eye of the thought-fox which approaches the watcher as 'a widening deepening greenness', and of 'the drills' of the jaguar's eyes, boring through the darkness of its captivity. We may want to explain what each animal represents, perhaps to say that the fox stands for inspiration, the jaguar for visionary powers, the goat for lawlessness; but although none of these interpretations is wrong, none is adequate. Fox, jaguar and goat represent instinct not reason; each is impressively mysterious; each makes us more inquisitive about what animals are, and about what they represent to our imagination.

Aesop's imaginative world is reassuringly clear about values; every story ends with a moral. Hughes's animal poems alarm some readers because they seem to advocate violence. There are poems in *Lupercal* which emphasise the law of the jungle — eat or be eaten — with a crispness which can sound appreciative:

> The crow sleeps glutted and the stoat begins.

> The tomcat still
> Grallochs odd dogs on the quiet,
> Will take the head clean off your simple pullet . . .

> Killers from the egg . . .

The first of these quotations is from 'Mayday on Holderness', which ends with thoughts of modern warfare, perhaps implying that killing is so inevitable in nature that it should not surprise or shock us in human affairs. The second, from 'Esther's Tomcat', evidently enjoys imagining the ruthless warrior skills of the old cat. The third sums up pike in 'Pike'. 'Hawk Roosting', as we have seen, speaks on behalf of the bird and presents an uncompromising manifesto: 'I am going to keep things like this.' We may admire the poem as an exercise on a theme. Suppose a hawk could speak: what would it say? Few modern writers would better Hughes's performance. Looking again at the relish with which Hughes performs here and in 'Pike' and the other examples, we may wish the poems offered more reassurance. There are hints of humour in 'Hawk Roosting' at the expense of the hawk's assumption that the world exists only for its convenience: 'The air's buoyancy and the sun's ray / Are of advantage to me; / And the earth's face upward for my inspection.' Are we intended to smile, or to be dismayed by the arrogance this represents? We cannot say.

Tennyson's 'Nature red in tooth and claw' is the phrase (see Part 1, pp.7–8, and Part 4, pp.67–72) which best summarises Hughes's unreassuring, unsentimental portrayal of animals. His poems about killers are effective at making the reader see how the killing is done. It is relatively easy to convey the monstrous appetite of the pike, with the grin which appears to be fixed in the fish's long jaw, and the cannibalistic habits implied in 'Pike', where one fish is half-buried in another. Hughes makes 'Thrushes' just as monstrous. His verbs catch the rapid, accurate action of the beaks in hauling worms out of the ground and dispatching them: 'drag', 'bounce', 'stab'. 'Relic' is a concise meditation on how every living creature in the sea is a predator: 'Nothing touches but, clutching, devours.' Hughes is equally effective in picturing dead animals. There is the massive dead pig in 'View of a Pig', where Hughes ponders the transition from warm-blooded life ('they feel like ovens') to cold meat. The sound of rain, heard as the speaker in 'Sunstroke' recovers consciousness, implies life; as he listens he sees the body of a fox which hangs from a beam, dangling as though killed in mid-jump. 'An Otter' ends with an abrupt change from images of the otter in its river ('Big trout muscle out of the dead cold' — where 'dead' stresses tenacity of life) to 'this long pelt over the back of a chair'. These examples are all from *Lupercal*. In later books Hughes has continued to emphasise violent death in nature. An extreme case among poems unsuitable for squeamish readers is 'February 17th' from *Moortown*. The dead lamb in this description is still jammed inside its mother, head sticking out; the job of extracting it ends only with its decapitation.

The beauty of animals is almost always accompanied by thoughts of mortality. 'A March Calf', from *Season Songs*, begins charmingly with the new-born 'Little Fauntleroy' in his best suit of black and white, 'shining-eyed' with an eagerness for life which the poem finds strange. Surely cattle ought by now to have learned what sort of world this is: 'people are getting hungrier' and butchers are 'developing expertise'. Also from *Season Songs* is 'A Cranefly in September', a poem which shows us the beauty of a familiar, clumsy insect, and reminds us of how the indifferent universe leaves it, 'tinily embattled', to its doom. 'Coming Down Through Somerset', from *Moortown*, pictures a dead badger's 'thrillingly painted face' and 'masterpiece skull' and records the poet's anguished regret as the body begins to decompose. Hughes's insistence on the fact of death is prevented from becoming morbid by his loving attention to detail in portraying living creatures. The same careful observation appears in other poems which dwell on the mystery of animals. This mystery can be terrifying, as in the last lines of 'Pike'. In 'Skylarks', from *Wodwo*, and 'Swifts', from *Season Songs*, the physical energy of the birds in flight seems magical. Elsewhere Hughes implies a faith — or, perhaps, an intimation — that there is a kind of knowledge quite different from ours. In 'Roe-Deer', from *Moortown*, there is a supernatural aspect to the 'secret deerhood', the experience of the wild which we cannot guess at, and knowledge which the poet would not understand even if the deer could speak to him. This leads us to another element in Hughes's work.

Myth

Prometheus is the only major classical figure who is identified by name, among the mythic personages in *Selected Poems*; the White Goddess lurks between the lines for those who wish to find her. (See Part 2, p.47 for details of how the Prometheus myth was treated by Aeschylus and Shelley.) Hughes's note on the poems from *Prometheus on His Crag* tells us that he combined the Greek stories with other material, and this is characteristic of Hughes's wish not to appear classical in the sense of being dependent on Greek and Latin culture. Readers who understand his Prometheus poems are helped by remembering the Greek myth, and readers who become seriously interested may use earlier literature to interpret them. A difficult line, for example, in Poem 9 of *Prometheus on his Crag* is 'The man I fashioned and the god I fashioned'. In some Greek versions of the legend Prometheus creates mankind; in others Zeus is the ruling deity who punishes Prometheus for helping mankind with the gift of fire stolen from heaven, and with instruction. Does Hughes mean that when Prometheus had made men from clay he 'fashioned' Zeus by teaching men, so that they came to invent religion? How would such a reading fit Shelley's interpretation in *Prometheus Unbound*? Shelley saw Prometheus as a Romantic rebel, aiding mankind in scientific, moral and political progress; Zeus, like every God in Shelley, is a tyrant obstructing man's proper development. This kind of 'literary' reading of poems in the light of earlier poems and classical myths, so often expected in the work of some major twentieth-century poets, including T.S. Eliot and W.B. Yeats (1865–1939), is not usually required in Hughes.

Discussions of his treatment of myth are complicated by the controversial nature of the term. *Myth* is a very complex word indeed. Some critics say that poets may create myth, by means of mythopoeic or myth-making imagination. Others hold that individuals cannot create myths but only adapt and redeploy such ancient stories as that of Prometheus. Hughes says that the stories of the Bible are myths. Some of those who agree with him would say that Bible stories and classical myths have different literary associations and are different in ethos. They might add that classical myths are different from myths which have never become part of Western culture. Hughes would argue that a truly modern poet writing in English makes no such distinctions, because Christian and classical traditions have lost their authority, even for traditional English readers, and for many in the English-speaking world of today these traditions never had any special authority anyway. Hughes's source for *Crow* was North American mythology: it was a 'trickster' (a type widely known to students of folk-lore) in the legends of the Winnebago Indians, a breaker of all taboos, a comic but disgraceful, outlawed but incorrigible being. Such an anti-hero, Hughes would say, is just as attractive to a modern poet as an imp or sprite or goblin.

He would agree that, whatever we think about myth, the test of such a mythic-seeming character as Crow, whatever his origins and analogues, is the success of the poems which try to bring him to life. The concluding Note in *Selected Poems* tells us that Crow appears in 'a sequence of poems relating the birth, upbringing and adventures of a protagonist of that name'. (It is implied that no other outside knowledge is needed; we find that some knowledge of Genesis is expected.) Crow combines the physical attributes of a bird with the shabby, furtive, scavenging characteristics of a common crow, and with supernatural powers. In 'Examination at the

Womb-Door' he is born into a world ruled by death, and here he asserts his only positive quality, the indestructibility which makes him 'stronger than death'. In 'A Childish Prank' and 'Crow's First Lesson' he intervenes in the creation as it is described in Genesis, and his foolery proves more effective than the muddled purposes of the God of Genesis. In 'That Moment' he survives the destruction of the world, still needing something to eat. How are we to place him? In the imaginative universe of the epic *Paradise Lost* (1667) by John Milton (1608–74), the most ambitious and successful poetic treatment in English of the Genesis stories, he would be a minor devil. Hughes has imagined a universe in which God and the devil have only illusory power, so that the most contemptible of mischief-makers can undo their work. Crow represents cosmic absurdity — all that remains for agnostic thinkers today of the traditional Christian scheme. In 'The Black Beast' he searches the cosmos for the devil. In 'A Horrible Religious Error' he swallows the serpent (which in Genesis represents the devil). Yet he is not quite absurd. He stands for a force in nature which is acknowledged throughout Hughes's writings; this is a mindless will to exist, which, Hughes believes, outlasts everything. In 'Crow's Last Stand' the whole creation is burned by the rage of the sun, except Crow's eye which stares on for ever. There is a bold simplicity to the invention which makes *Crow* appealing, at least on first encounter, and at best there is writing of the imaginative quality we know from earlier and later volumes:

God tried to teach Crow how to talk.
'Love,' said God. 'Say, Love.'
Crow gaped, and the white shark crashed into the sea
And went rolling downwards, discovering its own depth.

('Crow's First Lesson')

The bird's beak and the loveless godling's attempt to speak are fused in 'gaped': we feel how alien Crow is to the God of Love, and how independent the shark is of any creator in 'discovering its own depth'. More often the style is flatly colloquial, in a deliberate contrast to the grand poetic prose of Genesis:

So on the seventh day
The serpent rested.
God came up to him.
'I've invented a new game,' he said.

('Apple Tragedy')

Readers out of sympathy with Hughes's purpose may feel that bored schoolchildren have always scribbled such verses on fly-leaves in divinity lessons. The purpose was to find a style as drab as Crow himself, and to abandon the eloquence of biblical faith for the most unpretentious possible voice, fitting for contemporary myths in which there is no belief to be proud of. Hughes said in an interview (with E. Faas, 'Ted Hughes and Crow', see Part 5) that '*Crow* was really an idea of style . . . a super-simple and super-ugly language . . . the songs that a Crow would sing'.

Readers who have mixed feelings about *Crow*, or who think the sequence a failure, may prefer poems such as 'Wodwo', or 'How Water Began to Play', from *Crow*, which have an imaginative appeal as strong as folklore, but which do not demand to be interpreted in terms of Christianity or Buddhism or any large system of ideas. Both these poems grow in interest with rereading. Wodwo's delicately rambling phrases exist for the sake of the water-reeds, roots, stumps, leaves, water, frog, all of which are so much more real than he is, although his plain language gives him charm. The simple repetitions of 'How Water Began to Play', echoing the to-and-fro of running water, achieve a subtle, witty personification. Rock is brought to life in 'Still Life', from *Wodwo*, its thoughts—ignorantly smug —related to us in a voice of simple strong authority, appropriate for retelling or trying to create myth, but not always present in *Crow*. Other poems which, although not mythical in content, are mythopoeic in quality, include 'Fire-Eater', from *Lupercal*, which is difficult but worth wondering about.

People and places

Hughes has a strong sense of place and of how people belong to their environment. His Vikings in 'Thistles', from *Wodwo*, have grown into the British lands they conquered, where they reappear as thistles. Their physical looks and their personalities can be traced in the people too, in Yorkshire for example, according to 'For Billy Holt', from *Remains of Elmet* :

> The longships got this far. Then
> Anchored in nose and chin.

The colonel in 'The Retired Colonel' is the product both of a tough old England which has disappeared and of the foreign lands he helped to rule. The tramp found asleep in a ditch in 'November', also from *Lupercal*, has lived so much in the wet lanes of Devon that he is as fully at home there as a hedgehog and resembles one in his drawn-in face and sheltering hair. The moors of Devon where Hughes has lived and farmed for many years, and the Yorkshire moors west of Halifax where he spent his early childhood, are the two principal regions of his poems.

Devon appears as the background of many pieces from *Lupercal* on, but most effectively in the first sequence from *Moortown*. Onslaughts of winter and wintry-spring weather are described with great energy and obvious enjoyment in 'Tractor', 'Birth of Rainbow', 'Couples Under Cover' and 'February 17th'. Milder moments can be effective by contrast. 'Ravens' ends with a picture of a tranquil day in spring—the day on which the lamb of this poem has been still-born:

And its first day of death was blue and warm . . .
And the blackthorn budding confidently
And the skyline of hills, after millions of hard years,
Sitting soft.

The geological hardness of the millions of years is followed by softness which a painter might have seen in the landscape, and the metaphor treats the hills to the kind of rest a sheep-farmer enjoys after work; any effects of cosy prettiness in these closing lines are dispelled by the reminder of the lamb's fate. The farmers of Devon are glimpsed, respectfully and affectionately, in 'The Formal Auctioneer', where we see their sly faces concealing their intent at a cattle auction, and their quick, stealthy bids coming 'like night foxes'. 'Now You have to Push', which completes the Moortown sequence with a memorial to the poet's father-in-law, Jack Orchard, observes how a farmer whose whole life is spent working on the land is marked and weathered so that the countryside can be read in his hands and face.

The poems about people and places in Yorkshire show the sense of history to be seen in Hughes's prefatory note to *Remains of Elmet* (quoted in the note in Part 2, p.42), which comments on the decline of the Calder Valley. The wool trade and the coming of the Industrial Revolution in the eighteenth century made this a busy, active region; during Hughes's lifetime its traditional ways of life have gradually disappeared. Buildings such as the chapel in 'Mount Zion' remain as signs of the steadfast although harsh and narrow culture, dour in the chapels where 'Christ was only a writhen bleeding worm' and a child was marched to worship like a calf to slaughter, and hardened also by the 'sour hills' in a country with walls and roof of rain ('For Billy Holt'). This old Yorkshire can be admired and regretted, none the less. It had solid reliable virtues and a faith for which 'Heptonstall Old Church' finds a metaphor in a great bird whose song brought men to life 'out of rock' and 'out of bog and heather'. Now the dead bird has left its 'giant bones / Blackened' — perhaps in the form of abandoned buildings of dark millstone grit. In most of these poems human affairs are viewed in general terms and as though from a distance. A few names occur, such as that of Billy Holt, a 'character' famous in Yorkshire (although 'For Billy Holt' tells us nothing about him); 'Heptonstall Cemetery' names some of the dead, who are said to be 'feathers' in the 'giant beating wing' of the hillside in which they are buried, among them 'Sylvia'. In 'Emily Brontë' the poet-novelist's intense relationship with this part of England (see Part 2, p.45) is expressed in metaphors of physical love: 'The wind . . . was her darling', 'the curlew trod in her womb'. 'Football at Slack', by contrast, is a cheerful sketch of an everyday scene, and the earlier poem 'Her Husband', from *Wodwo*, portrays a grim Yorkshire marriage, husband and wife punishing each other for the poverty of their lives.

Another group of poems loosely connected with Yorkshire scenes has the theme of war, referring especially to the First World War, of which Hughes, the son of a survivor of the 1915–16 Gallipoli campaign, had heard horror stories since childhood. In 'Mayday on Holderness', from *Lupercal*, the poet contemplates the peaceful Yorkshire countryside where rivers run down to the North Sea, and intrudes thoughts of violence in nature, and thoughts of war. 'Six Young Men', from *Hawk in the Rain*, juxtaposes fresh young faces from a photograph with the fact that the soldiers have been buried for forty years; the sound of the waterfall in a Yorkshire valley connects the present moment with the day of the photograph. The place-names belong to London in 'Scapegoats and Rabies', from *Wodwo*; this poem begins with soldiers marching in a country lane and develops into a sequence of disconnected passages reflecting on twentieth-century death and destruction. People are usually impressive in Hughes's poems, despite poverty and hardship, while they are at work, especially when working on the land; they are least dignified and least natural (despite the poet's emphasis on violence in nature) at war.

Imagery

Descriptive writing in the poems is often startlingly vivid and memorable. The action of a jaguar's hip joint, the stirrings of the delicate legs of thrushes, the tilted hind-hooves of horses, the 'monstrous excess' of the legs of a cranefly (and its curly feet), the legginess of a new-born calf ('Half of him legs'), could be studied from Hughes's descriptions. Heads are just as carefully observed: an otter's is like a tom-cat's, a bull's is like masonry in the brow, a pike's long clamp-like hooked jaws were fixed in design for ever long ago and are perfect for their work. Words cannot exactly capture the sounds made by curlews, heard across marshes; it would be hard to get closer than 'Curlews Lift', from *Remains of Elmet*. Hughes finds words, too, for the warmth of a pig's skin, rubberiness of a cow's tongue, bristle of a badger's hair, bite of the seat in a frozen tractor, coolness of stone and iron in a barn, frost on a glass of wine, velvet of tarmac in a summer dawn, all the sensations of leaning into a dark byre to look at a bull, and hundreds of other sensory impressions. Any reader can make a longer list of favourites. The attempt to rehabilitate a reckling swift in 'Swifts', from *Season Songs*, would make a good example of the blending of precise and imaginative language, especially the abundance of forceful verbs, which gives descriptive writing in *Selected Poems* its power. A gift for simile and metaphor is noticeable there, and everywhere in the book.

Some images exaggerate in obvious ways which occur in everyday speech: a famous poet is out of touch with the young: he is 'a stegosaurus'. A water-drop on the kitchen wall is as old as the world, and so what a story

it could tell! It is addressed as 'Venerable elder!' in 'The Man Seeking
Experience Enquires His Way of a Drop of Water'. Images of this sort are
most frequent in the earliest poems. Others are appropriate but unremark-
able; we have probably seen them before: the old colonel's stiff behaviour
is 'like a last stand'; for Members of Parliament (in 'Wilfred Owen's Photographs', from *Lupercal*), changing the laws of the Navy would be like
losing their old school ties. But such dull figures of speech are rare.
Hughes is inventive in finding human likenesses for beasts and *vice versa*.
Parrots strut 'like cheap tarts'; deaf children, all eyes, are like lemurs, noc-
turnal monkeys. He enjoys Romantic comparisons: an otter crossing open
country away from its adopted element is 'like a king in hiding'; even better are some of his plainest: the hot-skinned pigs 'like ovens'. Some similes
discover physical comparisons for abstract qualities and states. 'It was as
deep as England', in 'Pike', compares the water in the pond and the age of
England, in the mind of the child fishing. The best images are surprising
and fitting. The fragile winter flower in 'Snowdrop', from *Lupercal*, is
admired for 'her pale head as heavy as metal'. The comparison is successful because it makes us consider how the snowdrop is able to break through
the frozen January ground.

For every simile there are a dozen metaphors; many of the best poems
are exercises in metaphor. The concrete is frequently substituted for the
abstract. In 'Bayonet Charge' a soldier runs, in his panic, as though

> To get out of that blue crackling air
> His terror's touchy dynamite.

In 'The martyrdom of Bishop Farrar', also from *The Hawk in the Rain*, the
dying bishop's words are coins, not legal tender but gold as good as Bloody
Mary's crown, for Protestants; smoke burns them into the sky. 'Gog',
from *Wodwo* begins beautifully with Gog's memory of waking to God's
cry: 'I ran and an absence bounded beside me.' The swifts have 'reduced
life' to a 'fine wire'. In the last words of 'An October Salmon', from *River*,
the fish dies 'patient / In the machinery of heaven'. There are other
changes of category. The skylarks sound human: 'Squealing and gibbering
and cursing.' They fly like aeroplanes and race like motorbikes. Sheep are
'petrified' in 'The Harvest Moon', from *Season Songs*; manes are 'stone'
in their stillness in 'The Horses', from *The Hawk in the Rain*. Machinery in
'Tractor', from *Moortown*, has a voice, 'Shouting Where Where?', and
when the engine warms, comes to life: 'Raging and trembling and rejoicing.'

Some poems are metaphorical throughout. 'Wind' unsteadies the world.
Its first stanza makes the house a storm-tossed ship; in the third stanza the
hills are tents pulling on guy-ropes; in the fifth the house is a goblet about
to shatter; in the last 'the roots of the house move'. 'October Dawn', also
from *The Hawk in the Rain*, develops thoughts about ice, which first shows

in delicate traces of autumn frost and has the power to halt rivers and crack the earth. Ice is a soldier, with a massive 'heave'; it gets 'its spearhead into place'. It is a smith, riveting and locking rivers. Mammoth and Sabre-tooth tiger, extinct since the last Ice Age, return in this poem. The first sign of them is just visible, in the October dawn, on a glass of wine. 'Still Life', from *Wodwo*, talks about 'outcrop stone' as though it were a miserly Yorkshireman, avoiding rent, playing dead, drawing interest from rain and snow, expecting to live for ever, unaware that in the blue of the short-lived harebell above it 'the maker of the sea' is sleeping, and waiting to erode the rock away. 'Apple Dumps', from *Season Songs*, contrasts lovely blossom with ailing apples from the same trees. The blossom was 'the fiesta, the beauty-contests, the drunken wrestling', the merriment, excitement, vanity, extravagance and irresponsibility of life. It was 'blushing and confetti', the wedding day. The apples are the tawdry prizes after the fiesta; they are hard-worked household hands and 'workworn morning plainness'. The blossom was religious hope, belied by the shoddy apples which remain. Such a poem is spoiled by prosaic explanation. It exists in its fresh, delicate images.

Hughes's confidence in the language of metaphor inspired poems such as 'The Green Wolf', about death. This poem does not tell us explicitly what its title means, that death is an evergreen hunter. It juxtaposes the plight of the neighbour in the first three stanzas, paralysed, while 'the dark blood-clot moves in', with the poet's impressions of how beauty and horror, life and death, are inseparable in nature:

                                        all
One smouldering annihilation
Of old brains, old bowels, old bodies
In the scarves of dew, the wet hair of nightfall.

'The Green Wolf' is the climax to a sequence of poems in *Wodwo*, beginning with 'Bowled Over', which do not attempt new ideas on a theme about which there is nothing new to say, but which find new images for the emotions death entails. The last section of 'Root, Stem, Leaf' pictures heirlooms, a girl's diary in a sale, or a lost spoon blackening in a hedge. 'Stations' notes the tulip-stalk at his door which outlives the dead man 'for a while'.

Hughes is bold with images, liking oxymorons, where the parts of an expression contradict each other, as in Milton's 'darkness visible': in 'West Laithe' gulleys are 'Cut in the cold fire'; his skylarks, weightless when settled, are 'leaden' in the sky, such is the solid mass of working muscle that lifts them. Some of his poems are experiments with fantasy. 'Ghost Crabs', from *Wodwo*, for example, is a venture into nightmare: the crabs come out of the sea and possess us, ruling our world invisibly. The poems from *Cave Birds* are more successfully surrealistic, although they suffer, in the setting of *Selected Poems*, without Baskin's accompanying pictures. 'The Knight' makes a bizarre, incongruous comparison, between a medieval knight's ideal of total submission to courtly discipline and the total abandonment to death of a decomposing crow. We may not accept Hughes's idea that consciousness sets humanity apart from all other creatures by causing feelings of rebellion against death. The poem is remarkable in blending culture and religion with images of the bird's crumbling body. The next poem, 'Bride and Groom Lie Hidden for Three Days', is equally strange in its metaphors of bodies as machines, and surprisingly effective.

'Wit' is the critical term for seventeenth-century English verse which makes an art of ingenious incongruity. Hughes is witty in that sense, and in his grim sense of humour. This is conspicuous in 'Do not Pick up the Telephone' (uncollected, *Selected Poems*, p.154), less easy to gauge elsewhere. 'Gnat-Psalm', from *Wodwo*, is attractive in its whimsy. The gnats are 'little Hasids', but also, delightfully pictured in a less dignified metaphor:

Dancing
Dancing . . .
Everybody everybody else's yoyo . . .

'Littleblood', from *Crow*, is an example of a witty though unfunny poem, serious but unsolemn, and so very much lighter in touch than *Crow*'s harsh jokes.

Versification

The poems from *The Hawk in the Rain* and *Lupercal* have more of the regularity of traditional verse than the later poems display, at least in terms of stanza form; the lines are usually irregular in the number of syllables and often irregular in the number of stresses. 'Famous Poet', for example, has uneven lines in stanzas of five lines, in each of which the first line and the last are joined and the intervening lines linked as a triplet by rhyme or half-rhyme, so that the rhyme scheme can be shown as *abbba*: 'remark' rhymes with 'dark', in the first stanza, and 'what' is a half-rhyme with 'that'. Hughes generally prefers the gently echoing effect of half-rhyme to rhyme, in those of the earlier poems which have stanzas in rhyming patterns. That is so in 'Meeting', for example, where the rhyme scheme links the three-line stanzas: *aba bcb cdc ded efe*. 'Witches' is as close as Hughes comes to regular lines—here lines of eight syllables, with four stresses, sometimes jauntily iambic:

Tŏ rĭde | ă wéed | thĕ rág | wŏrt róad

He does not submit long to such regularity of stress, however, even in this song. 'Relic', also from *Lupercal*, is exceptional in its reliance on rhyme for effects (although there is no regular rhyme scheme), especially in 'cold/hold' and in the concluding couplet.

Since *Wodwo* Hughes has written free verse, unaided by stanza, metre, rhyme — or in many poems from *Crow* and some later poems, by punctuation. 'How Water Began To Play' is a clear example of how successfully cadence verse can be written with only line endings and spacings of words and lines to mark intentions, and of how effective repetition can be. The opening of 'Tractor' is an example of disciplined lines where there is no obvious measure in the count of syllables, but where cadences make the line endings unalterable. Some lines in the later poems can be scanned in a conventional manner:

Shacklĕ pĭns | beddĕd ĭn | cast-ĭrŏn | cow-shĭt

These are exceptional, but no less effective in their contexts in poems as well composed as 'Tractor' — from which this comes.

Alliteration is a traditional poetic technique which Hughes has always employed. Early medieval English verse relies on strict schemes of alliteration before rhyme and syllable-count were adopted. Some poets feel that it is a technique natural to English verse. The obvious danger is a facile predictability: '*B*y the *b*ang of *b*lood in the *b*rain deaf the ear' ('The Jaguar'). 'Relic' is more interesting than that, trying to make the words click, grind and gnash like the jaws described. Assonance, the modulation of vowels, also plays its part: 'Slacken, go down jaws; go gnawn bare. Jaws'. Students can seek out for themselves examples which they like, and consider what makes the lines sound so well.

Part 4

Hints for study

TED HUGHES'S POEMS are best read aloud. He has made recordings of his readings (see Part 5), and you should listen to these if you can. Read the poems aloud to yourself, make your own recordings, and form a reading group with friends. Memorise the short poems which you like best, and recite them when nobody is about. Time spent this way is even more valuable than background study, necessary as that is.

Selected Poems has a small Baskin design on its cover, but it does not reproduce the Baskin engravings which illustrate *Crow* or those which should accompany *Cave Birds*. Ask about these in your library. You should make an effort to see Fay Godwin's photographs in *Remains of Elmet*, especially if you do not know Hughes's Yorkshire.

Some critical studies are recommended in Part 5. Not all those who have published commentaries on Hughes's work are helpful. Some of the selections from his later books have remained obscure even to professional critics. Hughes's advice would be to try to discover what is enjoyable in the poems before going on to try to puzzle them out.

The more you write, the better. There is a great difference between passive knowledge and active performance, between what you understand and what you can readily put into words. It is a bad mistake to spend long periods reading and taking notes and then to go into an examination without practice in writing. Writing helps to clarify ideas and to produce new ones. Having planned an essay you should sometimes write without consulting the notes you will have made, or with only skeleton notes, and without books. *Preparing For Examinations in English Literature*, in the York Handbooks series, gives further advice. One very useful hint is this: learn carefully the exact titles of the poems you will refer to in the examination. Hughes wrote 'Tractor' not 'The Tractor'; 'For Billy Holt' not 'Billy Holt'; 'Littleblood' not 'Little Blood'; 'Tiger-Psalm' not 'Tiger Psalm'; 'TV Off' not 'T.V. Off'. A little care of this kind will be well rewarded. (Many of the other candidates will be careless.) One last point is essential. Quotations must be accurate and no longer than necessary; and they must illustrate your points. Nothing is worse than the long, irrelevant, inaccurate quotations which fill many students' essays and exam-scripts.

The first of the essay questions which follow is treated in full, with specimen notes and guidance on preparation and a specimen answer based on the notes. For the second topic, notes and materials are provided as the starting points for a project which you may undertake. Titles of poems most likely to be useful are given for two of the remaining topics.

Essay questions

(1) Illustrate and discuss the theme of violence in *Selected Poems*.
(2) Discuss Hughes as a poet inspired by animals.
(3) Illustrate and discuss Hughes's poems on historical subjects.
(4) Illustrate and discuss Hughes's poems on the theme of death.
(5) Write about people in Hughes's poems.
(6) How does Yorkshire appear in the poems?
(7) Could you demonstrate from the poems that Hughes has first-hand knowledge of farming?
(8) In what sense is Hughes a witty poet?
(9) What has Hughes to say about life in the twentieth century?
(10) Write on the place of landscape in Hughes's poems.
(11) Write on Hughes's imagery.
(12) Write on Hughes's versification.

Treatment of essay questions

(1) Illustrate and discuss the theme of violence in *Selected Poems*.

Preparation

You might begin with the quotation from Tennyson's *In Memoriam* which is discussed in Part 1 (pp.7–8): 'Nature red in tooth and claw'. The next stage in preparing the essay is to consider what is obvious common ground even among those who disagree about the topic. Violence is a central theme in Hughes's work; he writes of violence in nature and of violence in human affairs. Make notes as follows:

(1) There are poems in the early volumes which depict strength joined with beauty in beasts and birds: 'The Thought-Fox', 'The Jaguar', 'The Horses', 'Meeting' (from *The Hawk in the Rain*); 'Esther's Tomcat', 'Hawk Roosting', 'The Bull Moses', 'An Otter', 'Thrushes', and 'Pike' (from *Lupercal*). The majority of these animals are presented as killers, often with an emphasis on the violence of their killing. Even among the peaceful animals there is a would-be aggression in the goat of 'The Meeting', and a latent threat in the bull, whose docility is regretted.

(2) Some of the best lines in these poems dwell on acts of dismembering, disembowelling, and so on.

> The tomcat still
> Grallochs odd dogs on the quiet . . .
>
> ('Esther's Tomcat')

> My manners are tearing off heads . . .
>
> ('Hawk Roosting')

> With a sag belly and the grin it was born with.
>
> ('Pike')

Such lines are remembered.

(3) Although violence is less apparent in animal poems in *Wodwo*, this theme returns, stronger than ever, in the poems from *Crow*. Crow creates the shark and the mosquito, attacks the serpent and eats it and is himself a scavenger. *Remains of Elmet* and the *Moortown* sequence involve less killing — prominence is given to the physical suffering of farm animals. 'Eagle', from *Under the North Star*, and 'Tiger-Psalm', from *Moortown*, are examples of how the theme persists in Hughes's later work. These two poems go further than 'Hawk Roosting' in imagining the point of view of the killer.

> Already the Fawn stumbles to offer herself up . . .
>
> ('Eagle')

> The tiger blesses with a fang.
>
> ('Tiger-Psalm')

(4) In poems which may be called mythical or surrealistic, 'The Executioner', a killer-hawk from *Cave Birds*, and the vulture which gnaws Prometheus, are typical symbols.

(5) Human affairs are violent in the majority of poems from the early volumes. 'Bayonet Charge' and 'Six Young Men' are war poems. Hughes was influenced by Wilfred Owen, whose involvement with war was forced upon him, since Owen was a serving soldier until his death in action. 'The Martyrdom of Bishop Farrar' is very good at using the physical details, in its description of a man being burned at the stake, to make its point that the bishop's protest was burned into the minds of the spectators.

> Out of his mouth, fire like a glory broke,
> And smoke burned his sermon into the skies.

Among poems from *Lupercal*, thoughts of war occur in 'Mayday on Holderness'; the 'Cold War' of the period following 1945 is the theme of 'A Woman Unconscious'. 'Wilfred Owen's Photographs' concerns flogging in the British Navy. 'The Retired Colonel' shows admiration for an irascible, tough old soldier and imperialist, in whose voice 'knout and whipcrack' can be heard. In 'Cleopatra to the Asp' the Queen is, on the point of suicide, vowing vengeance on Rome. Poems from *Wodwo* include 'Scape-goats and Rabies' and 'Out' on the theme of war. 'Thistles' and 'The War-riors of the North' are poems in appreciation—if not in praise—of the Vikings.

> Their sons appear,
> Stiff with weapons, fighting back over the same ground

('Thistles')

Use this example, because it illustrates Hughes's sense of fun.

We might select from later poems, 'A Motorbike', 'TV Off' and 'Tiger-Psalm', from *Moortown*, as examples of violence in human affairs; and add the extraordinarily bloody happenings in *Gaudete*, not apparent in the poems in *Selected Poems*.

(6) The novelist Graham Greene has observed that, in literature, 'an atmosphere of violence' may be more telling than the most outright descriptions of torture and carnage. In this sense many other poems might be brought within a discussion of violence in Hughes. This is especially true of poems from later volumes. We might want to give space to 'Stealing Trout on a May Morning' where images of battle burst into the calm of a spring day in the country and into the quiet mind of a fisherman. We might comment on the violence of the elements (the attack of the wind in 'Wind' on house and hills); or on the impression of life as a gruelling struggle, man in violent conflict with nature, in many of the poems from *Remains of Elmet* and *Moortown*.

The next stage is to think about interpretation. The question of violence has often been crucial in critical disagreements about the merit of Hughes's work. Some hostile critics think the poems excessively brutal. Admirers insist that Hughes is brave and realistic about the horror of existence and the violence of our time. Martin Seymour-Smith, for example, objects that *Crow* is based on 'a misunderstanding of the notion of "the survival of the fittest" . . . a reliance on the incorrect facts that "Nature" is all violence, cruelty, atrocity' (*A Guide to Modern World Literature*, 1973, p.344). Keith Sagar acknowledges that excesses of violence (mostly in work excluded from *Selected Poems*) are faults, but says that they 'fall away within the context of the overall, heroic tragic achievement' (*The Art of Ted Hughes*, 1975, p.146). We have to consider whether Hughes's nature is 'all violence'. We should consider, too, a charge which Hughes has tried to answer. Talking to an interviewer about 'Hawk Roosting' he said:

> That bird is accused of being a fascist . . . the symbol of some horrible totalitarian genocidal dictator. Actually what I had in mind was that in this hawk Nature is thinking. Simply Nature. It's not so simple maybe because Nature is no longer simple.

(*London Magazine*, January 1971)

The charge of 'fascist' can be used to connect poems such as 'Hawk Roosting', which exult in violence, although not in the poet's own voice, with others such as 'The Retired Colonel', from *Lupercal*, which admires the indomitable spirit of an old man who seems to have been the embodiment of all that British liberals most dislike, or 'A Motorbike', from *Moortown*, which implies that Britain in peacetime after 1945 was insupportably dull for those who had been soldiers during the war. Keith Sagar's claim that Hughes's achievement is 'tragic' in status cannot fairly be tested on the evidence of *Selected Poems* alone, but we should ask whether we find there the qualities of sympathy and imagination which raise works of literature to the level of tragedy. You may hold strong views which will cause you to write an essay more on one side or the other than the following sample, which tries to give a balanced view.

A specimen answer
Tennyson pictured Nature 'red in tooth and claw' (*In Memoriam*, LV). This is how Nature appears in many of Ted Hughes's best poems. He made his reputation with imaginative portrayals of jaguar, hawk and pike. His more recent 'Tiger-Psalm' proclaims the tiger as a lovely, natural killer: 'The tiger blesses with a fang'. In human affairs, too, there is an emphasis on killing, in the war poems and elsewhere. In the realm of the supernatural, Hughes's Prometheus 'began to admire the vulture' (*Prometheus on his Crag*, 10). Tennyson wrote with fear and horror of the shrieking of Nature against the creed that love is 'Creation's final law'. It is less easy to decide, reading Hughes's *Selected Poems*, how he regards violence.

A simple test of poetry is memorability. Which lines is a reader most likely to remember? Nobody will easily forget the words of Hughes's hawk in 'Hawk Roosting': 'My manners are tearing off heads.' Equally strong, plain and effective are the lines about Esther's tomcat who 'grallochs odd dogs on the quiet'. Those who do not know the word can guess what 'grallochs' means (disembowels) before looking it up. Looking at pike, ever after reading 'Pike', we will recall the 'sag belly' and 'the grin it was born with'. Hughes has passed these creatures through his imagination; by joining 'manners' so abruptly with the next phrase, the writing makes it seem that the hawk has a human satisfaction in its own ruthlessness. The cat's killing 'on the quiet' implies murder. 'Grin' is, of course, an illusion. There is a touch of humour lurking in all these examples — something alien to the beasts. *Crow* is memorable too, for its blend of colloquial English speech with mythic invention. 'Beat the hell out of it, and ate it': this is how Crow deals with the serpent of Genesis ('A Horrible Religious Error'). In 'Eagle', from *Under the North Star*, a more recent collection, the victims are visualised as eager sacrifices to an eagle which is not just a bird of prey but a killer-god. Hughes's mythological poems exult in thoughts of such wonders. 'The Executioner', from *Cave Birds*, is seen through the action of the fawn in 'Eagle': 'Already the Fawn struggles to offer herself up'. We shall remember that, and, in 'Tiger-Psalm', the line which seems to sanctify the tiger's slaying.

Hughes has employed his talent for conveying violent action in his poems about war: 'Bayonet Charge', from *The Hawk in the Rain*, and 'Scapegoats and Rabies', from *Wodwo*, for example. Many of his poems take subjects from history. 'The Martyrdom of Bishop Farrar', from his first book, makes us imagine a man being burned to death at the stake (in the religious persecution under Queen 'Bloody' Mary in the sixteenth century): 'see what / Black oozing twist of stuff bubbles.' The poem also makes a metaphor of the fire and smoke which burned the martyr's Protestant teaching, the last line says, into the skies of England. 'Thistles' is another excellent short poem inspired by history, this time by the Vikings, who also figure in 'The Warriors of the North', both from *Wodwo*. Thistles are or seem to be among the most aggressive of plants. 'Against' is the first word of the poem. Cows' tongues and farmers' hands are spiked by them. They are like this because they grow from an 'underground strain of a decayed Viking'. They resemble Vikings, pale, guttural, blood-plumed. When farmers mow them they start a blood-feud, as Vikings would have done: 'Their sons appear, / Stiff with weapons, fighting back over the same ground.' This is a pleasant, witty treatment of a phase of English history which was particularly bloodthirsty and which appeals to Hughes's imagination.

Such poems are fine performances. Their subjects are violent, but that is the case with much of the world's literature. It is because Hughes's work is so unremittingly devoted to animal and human ferocity that some readers have accused him of morbidity. Others have objected that 'Hawk Roosting' gives an appealing voice to the attitudes of fascism and that there are politically crude undertones in 'The Retired Colonel', 'A Motorbike', and other poems. To meditate on a decomposing crow may be morbid, although 'The Knight', from *Cave Birds*, which does so, is impressive none the less. Hughes's work is not for the squeamish or the sentimental. Literary criticism judges what is well written. 'Hawk Roosting', 'Thistles', 'The Knight' are, most critics will agree, more accomplished pieces of writing than some of the pieces in the 'Crow' sequence (and more intelligible than some from *Prometheus on his Crag* and *Adam and the Sacred Nine*). Critics may suspect that the thinking behind the poems is not always clear: 'Simply Nature . . . [but] Nature is no longer simple', said Hughes in an interview in 1971. Muddled thinking, however, can produce good poems, as sometimes happened with *In Memoriam*. To conclude with a personal judgment, poems such as 'Littleblood' and 'Wodwo', the short nature lyrics from *Remains of Elmet*, despite the atmosphere of violence in nature reminiscent of Emily Brontë, and the farming poems from *Moortown*, despite the physical details about lambing, come as a relief when one reads the whole volume through. Elsewhere there is too much of Nature red in tooth and claw and too little of her kinder moods.

(2) Discuss Hughes as a poet inspired by animals.

See the first section of Part 3. The idea of Hughes as 'a modern Aesop' must be used carefully, as a starting point. He does not write moral fables in the genre of Aesop. You may wish to explore the literary background further. You must read William Blake's 'The Tiger' (1794):

Tyger, Tyger, burning bright
In the forests of the night,
What immortal hand or eye
Could frame thy fearful symmetry?

In what distant deeps or skies
Burnt the fire of thine eyes?
On what wings dare he aspire?
What the hand dare seize the fire?

And what shoulder, and what art,
Could twist the sinews of thy heart?
And when thy heart began to beat,
What dread hand? and what dread feet?

What the hammer? What the chain?
In what furnace was thy brain?
What the anvil? What dread grasp
Dare its deadly terrors clasp?

When the stars threw down their spears,
And water'd heaven with their tears,
Did he smile his work to see?
Did he who made the Lamb make thee?

Tyger, Tyger, burning bright
In the forests of the night,
What immortal hand or eye,
Dare frame thy fearful symmetry?

This is symbolism. Blake used metaphors of the forge for his tiger's creation, and for its awesome mysterious creator, in order to raise the question of line 20. The poem is quoted here in full because Hughes's work so often brings it to mind. In contrast to Blake's pure symbolism, for example, 'The Jaguar' begins in a real zoo; the last line moves into a realm of the imagination, where the horizons race, comparable to the forests of the night. Blake's concentration and intensity are in contrast, however, to the repetitive wordiness of some of Hughes's work, including 'Tiger-Psalm'. Blake's tiger is made frightening without mention of claws or fangs.

Hughes must have been thinking of Shelley's 'To a Skylark' when he wrote 'Skylarks'; his poem's emphasis on the physical strength and energy of the birds is a deliberate contrast to Shelley's conception of a happy spirit:

> Hail to thee, blithe Spirit!
> Bird thou never wert,
> That from heaven or near it,
> Pourest thy full heart
> In profuse strains of unpremeditated art.

Shelley's archaism ('thou wert' for 'you were') and musical metre are another sort of contrast to Hughes's strictly modern English and free verse.

Tennyson's 'The Eagle' is an example of concentration and formal control. It creates drama and power within its six lines:

> He clasps the crag with crooked hands;
> Close to the sun in lonely lands,
> Ring'd with the azure world, he stands.
>
> The wrinkled sea beneath him crawls;
> He watches from his mountain walls,
> And like a thunderbolt he falls.

Hughes would say that even if a modern poet rivalled such technical accomplishment, the result would only echo the past: that is why he thinks it is better to write free verse.

Other examples provide other comparisons and contrasts. Here is D.H. Lawrence's 'Fish':

> But watching closer
> That motionless deadly motion,
> That unnatural barrel body, that long ghoul nose, . . .
> I left off hailing him.
>
> I had made a mistake, I didn't know him,
> This grey, monotonous soul in the water,
> This intense individual in shadow,
> Fish-alive.

Here is one of Hughes's models for his free verse, and a different approach to the subject of Hughes's 'Pike'. You might contrast these slight but appealing verses by Rupert Brooke (1887–1915):

> Unfading moths, immortal flies,
> And the worm that never dies.

> And in that heaven of all their wish,
> There shall be no more land, say fish.

The polished whimsy of these lines from 'Heaven' is typical of much early twentieth-century light verse. It is quite alien to Hughes. More comparable, in its metaphor and relish for animal power, is 'The Zebras' by Roy Campbell (1901–57):

> While round the herds the stallion wheels his flight,
> Engine of beauty volted with delight,
> To roll his mare among the trampled lilies.

---

(3) Illustrate and discuss Hughes's poems on historical subjects.

These are so many and various that they are best treated in order of composition: 'The Martyrdom of Bishop Farrar', from *The Hawk in the Rain*; 'Cleopatra to the Asp', from *Lupercal*; 'The Warriors of the North', from *Wodwo*, and the whole sequence from *Remains of Elmet* which treats Yorkshire history indirectly, are the best poems to choose for detailed comment. 'Strawberry Hill', 'Fourth of July' and 'Wilfred Owen's Photographs', from *Lupercal*, might be used in an additional paragraph: these are less interesting. 'A Woman Unconscious', 'The Retired Colonel' and some of the war-poems are historical in the sense of treating earlier twentieth-century subjects.

---

(4) Illustrate and discuss Hughes's poems on the theme of death.

T.S. Eliot's very well-known lines about the dramatist John Webster (*c*.1580–*c*.1625) would make a good introductory quotation:

> Webster was much possessed by death
> And saw the skull beneath the skin.
>
> ('Whispers of Immortality')

Hughes is much possessed by death. 'Six Young Men', from *The Hawk in the Rain*; 'Root, Stem, Leaf', 'Stations', 'The Green Wolf' and 'The Rat's Dance', from *Wodwo*; 'Heptonstall Cemetery', from *Remains of Elmet*; 'Life is trying to be Life' and 'The Stone', from *Moortown*, are the best poems to discuss, or at least to mention.

Part 5

Suggestions for further reading

The text

HUGHES, TED: *Selected Poems 1957–81*, Faber, London, 1982; available in paperback. This is the text used in the preparation of these Notes.

Selected works by Ted Hughes

Poems
The Hawk in the Rain, Faber, London, 1957.
Lupercal, limited edition, Turret Books, London, 1966.
Wodwo, Faber, London, 1967.
Crow: From the Life and Songs of the Crow, Faber, London, 1970; second edition with seven additional poems, 1972; limited edition illustrated by Leonard Baskin, with three additional poems, 1973.
Selected Poems 1957–67, Faber, London, 1972.
Prometheus on His Crag, limited edition, Rainbow Press, London, 1973.
Cave Birds, limited edition, with drawings by Leonard Baskin, Scolar Press, London, 1975; revised edition, as *Cave Birds: An Alchemical Cave Drama*, with drawings by Leonard Baskin, Faber, London, 1978.
Season Songs, illustrated by Leonard Baskin, Viking Press, New York, 1975; Faber, London, 1976.
Gaudete, Faber, London, 1977.
Orts, limited edition, Rainbow Press, London, 1978.
Moortown Elegies, limited edition, Rainbow Press, London, 1978.
Adam and the Sacred Nine, limited edition, Rainbow Press, London, 1979.
Moortown, Faber, London, 1979; includes poems from *Prometheus on His Crag*, *Orts*, *Moortown Elegies* and *Adam and the Sacred Nine*.
Under the North Star, with drawings by Leonard Baskin, Faber, London, 1981.
River, with photographs by Peter Keen, Faber, London, 1983.
Flowers and Insects, with drawings by Leonard Baskin, Faber, London, 1986.

Adaptations
Seneca's Oedipus, adapted by Ted Hughes, Faber, London, 1969.
AMICHAI, YEHUDA: *Selected Poems*, Penguin, Harmondsworth, 1971 (from the Hebrew, with Assia Gutmann and Harold Schimmel).
PILINSZKY, JANOS: *Selected Poems*, Carcanet, Manchester, 1976 (from the Hungarian, with Janos Csokits); with an introduction by Ted Hughes.

Prose writings
Introduction to Keith Douglas: *Selected Poems*, Faber, London, 1964.
Introduction to *A Choice of Emily Dickinson's Verse*, Faber, London, 1968.
Poetry in the Making: An Anthology of Poems and Programmes, Faber, London, 1969.
Introduction to Vasko Popa: *Collected Poems 1943–1976*, Carcanet, Manchester, 1977.
'Myth and Education', *Children's Literature in Education*, 1, 1970, pp.55–70.

Books for children
Hughes is a prolific and distinguished writer in this genre. Here are a few suggestions.
Meet My Folks!, poems, illustrated by George Adamson, Faber, London, 1961.
Nessie the Mannerless Monster, a narrative poem, illustrated by Gerald Rose, Faber, London, 1964.
The Iron Man: A Story in Five Nights, illustrated by George Adamson, Faber, London, 1968.
Moon-Whales, illustrated by Leonard Baskin, Viking Press, New York, 1976.

Recordings
The Poet Speaks, No. 5, Argo PLP 1085. Recorded 1963. Hughes introduces and then reads 'Her Husband', 'Bowled Over', 'Still Life', 'Wodwo', 'Mountains', 'The Warriors of the North', 'Gog', 'Out', 'Full Moon and Little Frieda' (in a longer version than that in *Selected Poems*).
Jupiter Anthology of 20th Century English Poetry, Part III, Jupiter JUR 00A8. Recorded 1963. Hughes reads 'The Hawk in the Rain' and 'Hawk Roosting'.
The Poetry and Voice of Ted Hughes, Caedmon TC 1535, Teakfield Distributors, 1977. Hughes reads 'The Thought-Fox', 'The Jaguar', 'Wind', 'Six Young Men', 'Mayday on Holderness', 'The Retired Colonel', 'View of a Pig', 'Sunstroke', 'Pike', 'An Otter', 'Hawk Roosting', 'Bride and Groom Lie Hidden for Three Days' and a few poems not included in *Selected Poems*.

Ted Hughes and R.S. Thomas, The Critical Forum, Norwich Tapes Ltd., Markfield House, Caldbec Hill, Battle, Sussex. Hughes reads and comments on six poems from *Moortown*.

Critical studies

BOLD, ALAN: *Thom Gunn and Ted Hughes*, Oliver and Boyd, Edinburgh, 1976.

FAAS, EKBERT: *Ted Hughes: The Unaccommodated Universe*, Black Sparrow Press, Santa Barbara, 1980. Includes interviews with Hughes, notably that for the *London Magazine*, January 1971, pp.5-20.

GIFFORD, TERRY and ROBERTS, NEIL: *Ted Hughes: A Critical Study*, Faber, London, 1981.

HAMILTON, IAN: 'A Mouthful of Blood', *Times Literary Supplement*, 8 January 1971, reprinted in *A Poetry Chronicle*, Faber, London, 1975. This is an able attack on *Crow*.

HIRSCHBERG, STUART: *Myth in the Poetry of Ted Hughes*, Wolfhound Press, Portmarnock, County Dublin, 1981.

HOLBROOK, DAVID: 'The Crow of Avon? Shakespeare, Sex and Ted Hughes', *Cambridge Quarterly*, Volume 15, 1986, pp.1-12. Hostile to Hughes.

LODGE, DAVID: 'Crow and the Cartoons', *Critical Quarterly*, Volume 13, Spring 1971, pp.37-42 and 68.

ROBERTS, NEIL: 'Ted Hughes and the Laureateship', *Critical Quarterly*, Volume 27, Summer 1985, pp.3-5.

SAGAR, KEITH: *The Art of Ted Hughes*, Cambridge University Press, Cambridge, 1975; second edition, revised and enlarged, 1978.

SAGAR, KEITH (ED.): *The Achievement of Ted Hughes*, Manchester University Press, Manchester, 1983. Includes 'Hughes and England', an essay by Seamus Heaney.

SEYMOUR-SMITH, MARTIN: *A Guide to Modern World Literature*, Macmillan, London, 1973, 1975. His account of Hughes is lively and very hostile.

SMITH, STAN: critical essay on Hughes in *Contemporary Poets*, fourth edition, edited by James Vinson and D.L. Kirkpatrick, St James Press, London, 1985.

WALDER, DENNIS: *Ted Hughes*, 'Open Guides to Literature', Open University Press, Milton Keynes, 1987. This is a readable and intelligent short study, intended for beginners.

WEST, THOMAS: *Ted Hughes*, 'Contemporary Writers', Methuen, London, 1984. This is a useful introduction.

The author of these notes

NEIL MCEWAN was educated at Pembroke College, Oxford. He has taught at the universities of Alberta, Leeds, Yaoundé and Fez, and at present lectures on English literature at the University of Qatar. He has published several critical studies, including *The Survival of the Novel*, *Africa and the Novel*, *Perspectives in British Historical Fiction Today*, and *Graham Greene* (1988) in the series 'Macmillan Modern Novelists'. He has also written *Preparing for Examinations in English Literature* and *Style in English Prose* in the York Handbooks series, and York Notes on L.P. Hartley: *The Go-Between*, Henry James: *Daisy Miller* and *The Europeans*, D.H. Lawrence: *Women in Love*, and Evelyn Waugh: *Decline and Fall*.